AN INSPIRATION TO EVERYONE
WHO WORKS WITH CHILDREN—
A GREAT HUMAN STORY!

"What comes out of the book is an extraordinary ferment,
a bubbling, bursting surge of life . . . born of instinct,
experience and love . . . Probably one of the most seminal
books ever written on the subject of a teacher's experience. Unconventional, impressionistic, instinct with passion, it may cause the hair of some pedagogues to stand
on end. But what happened in the classroom—called the
"infant room"—of the provincial New Zealand school
where Sylvia Ashton-Warner taught five-year-old Maori
and white children for twenty-four years might, in its
modest way, start a change in human development that
could revolutionize the world."

—Virgilia Peterson, **Newsday**

TEACHER

TEACHER

by Sylvia Ashton-Warner

BANTAM BOOKS
TORONTO · NEW YORK · LONDON

*This low-priced Bantam Book
has been completely reset in a type face
designed for easy reading, and was printed
from new plates. It contains the complete
text of the original hard-cover edition.*
NOT ONE WORD HAS BEEN OMITTED.

TEACHER
*A Bantam Book / published by arrangement with
Simon & Schuster, Inc.*

PRINTING HISTORY

Simon & Schuster edition published September 1963

2nd printing . September 1963		4th printing ... October 1963
3rd printing . September 1963		5th printing .. December 1963

Grade Teacher Book Club edition published February 1964

Bantam edition / October 1964

2nd printing ...... July 1965	8th printing .. February 1970
3rd printing ... January 1966	9th printing .. February 1970
4th printing ... October 1966	10th printing . September 1971
5th printing .... August 1967	11th printing ..... May 1972
6th printing ... October 1968	12th printing .. October 1973
7th printing .... March 1969	13th printing .. October 1974
14th printing .... November 1975	

ISBN 0-553-11327-5

Published simultaneously in the United States and Canada

---

*Bantam Books are published by Bantam Books, Inc. Its trade-
mark, consisting of the words "Bantam Books" and the por-
trayal of a bantam, is registered in the United States Patent
Office and in other countries. Marca Registrada. Bantam
Books, Inc., 666 Fifth Avenue, New York, New York 10019.*

PRINTED IN THE UNITED STATES OF AMERICA

0 9 8 7 6 5

To
Robert Gottlieb

Contents

TEACHER

Preface

This is an important book—as important as any book can be at this point in history. Miss Ashton-Warner believes that she has discovered a method of teaching that can make the human being naturally and spontaneously peaceable. Aggressiveness, an "instinct" without which wars could not arise or be conducted, is the name we give to mental or emotional reactions caused by the frustration of the child's inherited drives: self-preservation and sexual gratification. Education as normally practised throughout the world ignores these main interests. By recognizing and even welcoming their presence in the child and making them the foundation of an "organic" method of teaching, these interests can be allowed expression and be at the same time moulded into patterns of constructive delight. Destructiveness and creativity are opposed forces in the life of the mind. To create is to construct, and to construct cooperatively is to lay the foundations of a peaceful community.

As a prognosis of our social ills, such ideas are not new. They are implicit in the psychological revelations of Freud and Jung, and their disciples have accumulated the clinical evidence till it is an unanswerable indictment of our civilization. But how do we begin to cure ourselves of this universal neurosis? The author of this book has the answer: begin in the infant room (I would say begin even earlier, but so long as the mind of the infant is still malleable, it is not too late).

There are many possible approaches to creative education, but they all usually fail because they are too intentional, too self-consciously applied (the "self" being the teacher). Miss Ashton-Warner has realized that teaching is an organic process. She defines the necessary attitude of the teacher and gives a practical demonstration of an effective method of teaching. The teacher must possess or cultivate "negative capability," that quality which Keats thought was necessary in a poet. He or she must be there, in the infant room, solely for the purpose of calling on the child's own resources, which in practice means that she must have the patience and wisdom to listen, to watch and wait, until the individual child's "line of thought" becomes apparent. This "line" may be crooked—in its first years the child develops a mental complex of guilt as naturally as it inherits the physical traits of its parents. But these unconscious forces determine the *intensity* of its interests, and learning becomes incomparably easier if it is built on such a dynamic basis—in fact, it becomes part of the unfolding pattern of personality, as inevitable, in the author's words, "as a law of physics."

The teacher's duty, then, is merely to set the creative pattern into which these forces will then naturally flow. This, of course, is not a new idea—in fact, it is as old as Plato. But mankind has never had the desire or intelligence to apply such an insight to the process of education. It can be applied, however, and this book demonstrates how, step by step, it was applied in a particular community.

I have not had the good fortune to meet any of the Maori children taught by Miss Ashton-Warner, but the stories which she tells in the second half of the book bring them very vividly before us. The author has a wonderful gift of narrative, as she has already shown in her successful novel *Spinster*. The same gift is again evident. But . . .

But her reports are factual, and this new book is a sociological document rather than a pedagogical treatise. It is nevertheless intensely moving and should have a beneficial effect on teaching everywhere. I say "teaching" rather than "education," for education has long ago lost its proper meaning (which is exactly what Miss Ashton-Warner is advocating—a drawing out of another's mind). The school should be conceived, in the author's phrase, as "a crèche of living where people can still be changed," and where creative activities are the agents of this change. If we want humanity to have a future—a future of any

12

kind—*this is all that matters*. That is why I say that this book, however unprofessional or unacademic it may seem, is a book of fundamental significance. Without exaggeration it may be said that the author has discovered a way of saving humanity from self-destruction. We should not ignore her method because it is so unassuming, so unpretentious. Great changes in the destiny of mankind can be effected only in the minds of little children.

HERBERT READ

"What a dangerous activity reading is; teaching is. All this plastering on of foreign stuff. Why plaster on at all when there's so much inside already? So much locked in? If only I could get it out and use it as working material. And not draw it out either. If I had a light enough touch it would just come out under its own volcanic power. And psychic power, I read in bed this morning, is greater than any other power in the world. What an exciting and frightening business it would be: even that which squeezes through now is amazing enough. In the safety of the world behind my eyes, where the inspector shade cannot see, I picture the infant room as one widening crater, loud with the sound of erupting creativity. Every subject somehow in a creative vent. What wonderful design of movement and mood! What lovely behaviour of silksack clouds!

"An organic design. A growing living changing design. The normal and healthful design. Unsentimental and merciless and shockingly beautiful."

—SPINSTER

Seven Years After: An Introduction

I do not "recollect in tranquillity" seven years after.

I thought that in looking back on my work in that volcanic prefab, either I would see it in benign indulgence or, at least, frozen in perspective, I would see nothing but masses of vast mistakes and would wish to overhaul the whole thing, but neither of these things happens. I find I am not indulgent, neither have I perspective. I am touched with the fever of it all over again and am swept up in its drama; the drama in the bloodstream when people are real, of grownups as well as children.

There is, however, in the following pages, something left out: I didn't talk about discipline. An overall reflection of that work in the prefab could well give teachers a valid suspicion of chaos with the freedom of movement and talk. But chaos has a certain quality of its own that none of us allows in teaching; chaos presupposes a lack of control, whereas control was my first intention. As my inspector at that time observed, "Discipline is a matter of being able to get attention when you want it."

I often wanted attention and I wanted it smartly. And I trained the children in a way that is new only, maybe, in degree. Most teachers have some simple way of calling a room to attention; some use a bell, some rap a ruler, and most, I should think, use their voices. But where the sounds of learning and living are allowed in a room, a voice would need to be lifted and sharpened and could be unrepresentative of a gentle teacher; so, predictably, I used the keyboard. No crashing chord, no alarming octave, but eight notes from a famous master: the first eight notes from Beethoven's Fifth Symphony. What was good enough for him was good enough for me, since, whereas he demanded attention for the rest of the symphony from several thousand people, I wanted it for only a sentence. Here are these memorable notes.

At the sound of these notes I trained the Little Ones, whatever they were doing, to stop and look at me. I trained them this way from necessity but in time I did so from pleasure. And never through those vital years in the heaving prefab did I cease to be impressed at the sudden draining away of sound, like blood from a face, into the utmost silence. And not just silence but stillness; every eye on me, every hand poised; an intensity of silence born from sound . . .

For me to speak and be heard by all.

Some simple direction, some needed advice indisputably heard by all.

How I polished this instrument of attention! My most valuable too, the most indispensable of them.

For it is not so much the content of what one says as the way in which one says it. However important the thing you say, what's the good of it if not heard or, being heard, not felt? To feel as well as hear what someone says requires whole attention. And that's what the master's command gave me—it gave me whole attention. You might argue, "But how could a child at the far end of a room full of movement, talk and dance hear eight soft single notes?" Any teacher could answer that. The ones near the piano did. And they'd touch the others and tell the others until the spreading silence itself would tell, so that by the time the vibration of the strings had come to rest, so had the children. Those silences and those stillnesses, I'll remember them . . . for more than seven years after.

This is a good place to acknowledge the letters and visits from New Zealand teachers over the time between, and the interest and action of universities overseas. Thank you very much. I would dearly have loved to teach you on the spot at that time with the prefab as it was then as a center. I used to wish in my own wild way that you could have boarded and camped in the district in groups and come to us each day. But wishes, though wild, can be modest as well, and things did not work out that way. However, wishes can also be remarkably enduring and these remain with me seven years after.

I have not reread this Creative Teaching Scheme.

No doubt if I did risk it I should see the need to reconstruct, reorganize, rewrite, even rethink, but I mean to do none of these things. This is how it was when I wrote it and how it was when I worked it and it was all right for me as it was.

Besides, who would disturb a memory . . . the glamour of a moment in time? And who cares to resurrect the passion of the past? It is quite enough to recall what I have. As the living teacher teaches and, having taught, moves on, so

> *The Moving Finger Writes; and, having writ*
> *Moves on: nor all your Piety nor Wit*
> *Shall lure it back to cancel half a Line,*
> *Nor all your Tears wash out a Word of it.*

SYLVIA ASHTON-WARNER

Letter to
My American Editor

DEAR BOB,

You have asked me in your letter this morning to expand the introduction above, but I cannot on three accounts. That introduction was written for a hoped-for publication of my work in my country by a New Zealander with passion and energy . . . but it has failed like all the others. It was an introduction for my own country, but one for your country is another thing. Then again, when an artist is at work on material the ideas are hot and fluid, they have adjustability and temperature, like the astronomical gases in the universe, receptive to any shape that forces impose. But once time has set them in a shape . . . a cold impersonal star . . . their form is unchanging . . . final. The last reason is much more earthy; I can't since it makes me cry.

But I can still answer some of your questions. "A few cool facts" you want for your American readers. "When did it happen?" is the first you ask.

It began . . . how long ago? When I first put my young nose in a Maori infant room. Let me see . . . four, eight . . . four and eight are twelve . . . and four is sixteen . . . and four is twenty . . . and four is twenty-four; twenty-four years ago. Can it be so long? And it ended seven years ago when I at last came upon the Key Vocabulary. Or shall I say it came upon me? The revelation was brilliant, like lightning . . . I saw the tables with the scratches and stains, the bare boards on the floor and the undressed rafters. All lit with the white of lightning. . . .

What were my circumstances? . . . you've got them here. That question should be answered in the diary at the end.

How long? you ask. I've said so . . . twenty-four years. How many children? Nine or ten at the start, I think, swelling to seventy at one school in the spring, and something under fifty in the prefab when I saw the Key Vocabulary.

Then you say, "And if you can bear to, some narrative about how your ideas developed, and what the effect of them has been on New Zealand Education. I think this is important to our public here—*please* don't back away. (Also—something about how they have been received in New Zealand.)" Do you hear this sigh across the Pacific?

How my ideas developed? I don't know. I don't know that ideas do develop. They just appear. We marvel at them and are grateful, and that's all there is to it. As for the rest of that question . . . the reception of my work in New Zealand . . .

A family. That's what a small country can be, a family. In New Zealand we are more tightly and tensely a family than most small countries, owing to the southern oceans all round us . . . and being underneath the world to boot, and in all real families there is loyalty. Some families quarrel and some families don't, but in a real family there is a law, both clearly written and spoken, that no member speaks outside of it of what goes on inside it; a matter of dignity as well as loyalty.

A woman said to me once so proudly, "My family never quarrels." I was young at the time and our children were young and I thought "How wonderful! If only I could say that." But I'm not young now and I know better. When I look back on that family who never quarrelled I remember their passivity; the slow eyes that did not flash; on the parents' faces, no grooves that tears had scoured. I know now that it takes passion and energy to make a quarrel . . . of the magnificent sort. Magnificent rows, magnificent reconciliations; the surging and soaring of magnificent feeling.

We quarrel in New Zealand. Take that straight. We quarrel morning and afternoon, day and night. We quarrel from left to right and from right to left; from front to back and from back to front; from top to bottom, from bottom to top; from side to side and corner to corner . . . an highly complex, intricate, sparking, perorating, exhausting network of the most accomplished, nonstop cross-quarrelling that ever fired the blood of a country. And that's how it will continue to be until our red-hot, bright-eyed, pioneer corpuscles achieve some kind of dilution. For there is passion and energy here, brilliances and heroisms every morning (as regularly as the morning paper) challenging and piercing the alarmed mediocrities; generating all manner of sensational ideas that collide and explode like astral galaxies . . . like galaxies of southern stars. . . .

We quarrel, Bob. I can imagine no country living so erroneously with so much delighted confidence. But we don't talk outside our family. We're as timelessly loyal as the Southern Cross itself and obey all the timeless rules. So there are some things you ask me that I cannot answer.

It is true that I have been trying to get this Creative Teaching Scheme published in my country for seven eventful years. I kept it here these seven years, trying, hoping, waiting, crippled with family loyalty. I stubbornly wanted it to come out in my own country in my own lifetime . . . not after. I wanted to be here to see it; selfishly and vainly I wanted to see it. I wanted to train the teachers myself. How I longed to see some of these crack New Zealand infant mistresses here get hold of this thing and operate it; coolly without my creative fever, efficiently without my crises. Not that the teachers themselves did not want it: its principles, found briefly and inadequately in *Spinster*, have been used widely throughout the country, which I appreciated indeed. But one publisher said the style wouldn't do, that I'd have to remodel it on more orthodox lines; a . . . b . . . c . . . sort of thing; first things first and so on; he wanted to organize me in sober pedestrianism. Another publisher said, believe it or not, and he put this down on paper . . . "I can't. . . . It's before its time." Another kept it for a year and said nothing until, when I asked for it back, he burst into brilliant protest that I hadn't given him a chance to read it. "Can't you leave it for the weekend?" Another said he couldn't afford it, which was true. Somewhere along the line . . . at the very start, I think . . . I sent it to the Education Department itself, but a man there kept it for three months with no answer, and when I wrote and asked for it back, he said there had been no covering letter. (There was.) He remarked most graciously that he found it interesting and sincerely hoped I would receive it back safely. I can't help laughing putting this down; it reads like one of the tall stories I used to make up for my Little Ones. Not to mention the attempt of a good friend of mine down here to publish it this year, purely to please me; during the course of which the printing press, after pulling one copy from the machines, collapsed financially and emotionally, folded up and lost the type-set anyway, which has not been found to this day. After all of which, to put it mildly, I took a second look at family loyalty.

As for your question about how New Zealand Education received it . . . how they treated me through the years of experiment . . . what happened when I began operating it . . . what they did to me then . . . my Gethsemane . . . and later when *Spinster* came out . . .

Not that I blame New Zealand for conditions unfavourable to art. There's no such thing beneath the heavens as conditions favourable to art (much less to obsessional art). Art must crash through or perish, and I simply just crashed through; but not without wounds, believe me. Take what you want from life, but pay for it in blood. I took what I wanted . . . and paid. But all that's an in-family, in-country drama that I will not and cannot speak of, inside or outside my country, inside or outside yours, till a grave in New Zealand cools me. Then my spirit will rise before its time, to haunt them and speak the unspeakable. Remember what I say.

So here is my work in your country; my life's work before your readers. I send it to the teachers who have written to me, the wives, the journalists, the reviewers, the professors in the universities, above all to my elegant spinsters. They have sent to me in their letters the best of themselves. I send the best of myself. Some of them will agree with me and some of them won't, but I've learnt from experience that those who won't will criticize with intelligent charity. Note those two words: intelligence and charity. With the spotlight on the last word . . . charity. I've had some strong criticism in your country at times, but my blood never halted in shock; each pen was dipped in charity.

I'm sending the Creative Teaching Scheme from my country to yours, Bob, because I believe it is important. As Anna Vorontosov said in *Spinster,* "I must do what I believe and I believe in what I do; life is too short for anything else." I believe it is universal. For black, for white, for yellow and brown . . . it is universal. With tragic and desperate application to the racial minorities learning another culture.

There is one question you have not asked: Where are the books I made that I talk about all the time? I began making them that first week twenty-four years ago; writing, drawing, testing, discarding, improving, testing, rejecting; testing, improving, testing, improving; drawing endless pictures, hundreds of paintings . . . illustrating through the years until, seven years ago, as you will see in my diary, I took them to a bookbinder to bind them for me. He made a lovely job of them, in hard covers. Book One was yellow, Book Two was blue, Book Three was green and Book Four was red; across one top corner of each was a bright Maori rafter pattern and each cover had a figure of the central character, a little Maori boy with his singlet and pants failing to meet . . . a different pose on each cover. The pages were stiff white Whatman to take the hundreds of water-colour illustrations, and the text in large children's type. And it seemed to me at that time . . . although now, looking back, not quite . . . to at least come within striking distance of the dream, something anyway to begin on. I called them the Transition Readers. However, after all that, there comes another story of in-family drama not to be told outside. Until there came a day when I read in a letter that my Transition Books had been burnt. By mistake . . . but not by me.

I started again almost at once and got two nearly done but they were not the same and I stopped. I no longer had the same inclination, neither had my hand the same precision, which had nothing to do with age. It's true that I showed this new one to a publisher here . . . after

I had resigned from teaching . . . but it was plain I had too many colours. They suggested I reduce them to two, or at least to the primary colours, which I could see was quite right and reasonable . . . it's just that I'm not always reasonable. They gave a lot of their time and good thought to it, and had a page priced overseas . . . but this page turned out to cost £65. So they really could do no more. And this large book with more colours than Joseph's coat . . . this book of echoes . . . it lies on my shelf to this day. Lurks on my shelf I should say. Anyway I was not much of an artist.

"A few cool facts" you asked me for . . . I don't know that there's a cool fact in me, or anything else cool for that matter, on this particular subject. I've got only hot long facts on the matter of Creative Teaching, scorching both the page and me.

I have been writing to you in pencil by the fire with the evening to myself. Meaning to correct, revise, improve, and type—and shorten—don't forget . . . tomorrow. But I can't do any of these things. I'm going to tear these pages out of this notebook and put them in an envelope tomorrow, to be posted over the Pacific . . . never to read again. Don't fear they are too rough to publish; with or without punctuation and polish; backwards, upside-down or downside-up my readers will know what I mean.

So good luck with this, and thank you. I am glad it is over. And don't ever ask me to do anything so hard again. But I feel better . . . as I was before I began twenty-four years ago. I feel that with this letter going to you—the roughest bit of prose I have ever allowed to go to press —and with my Creative Teaching Scheme going to readers that know what I'm talking about . . . I feel my life's work is over. And I know what it means to rest.

With love,

SYLVIA

Creative Teaching

Organic Reading Is Not New

Organic reading is not new. The Egyptian hieroglyphics were one-word sentences. Helen Keller's first word, "water," was a one-word book. Tolstoy found his way to it in his peasant school, while, out in the field of UNESCO today, it is used automatically as the only reasonable way of introducing reading to primitive people: in a famine area the teachers wouldn't think of beginning with any words other than "crop," "soil," "hunger," "manure," and the like.

Not that organic reading is exclusively necessary to the illiterate of a primitive race. True, it is indispensable in conducting a young child from one culture to another, especially in New Zealand where the Maori is obliged to make the transition at so tender an age; but actually it is universal. First words are different from first drawings only in medium, and first drawings vary from country to country. In New Zealand a boy's first drawing is anything that is mobile; trucks, trains and planes, if he lives in a populated area, and if he doesn't, it's horses. New Zealand girls, however, draw houses first wherever they live. I once made a set of first readers on these two themes. But Tongan children's first drawings are of trees, Samoan five-year-olds draw churches and Chinese draw flowers. What a fascinating story this makes!

How can anyone begin any child on any arranged book, however good the book, when you know this? And how good is any child's book, anyway, compared with the ones they write themselves? Of course, as I'm always saying, it's not the only reading; it's no more than the *first* reading. The bridge.

It's the bridge from the known to the unknown; from a native culture to a new; and, universally speaking, from the inner man out.

Organic reading is not new: first words have ever meant first wants. "Before a nation can be formed," says Voltaire, "it is necessary that some language should be established. People must doubtless have begun by sounds, which must have expressed their first wants. . . . Idioms in the first state must have consisted of monosyllables. . . .

"We really find that the most ancient nations who have preserved anything of their primitive tongue still express by monosyllables the most familiar things which most immediately strike the senses. Chinese to this very hour is founded upon monosyllables.

"The Chaldeans for a long time engraved their observations and laws upon bricks in hieroglyphics: these were speaking characters. . . . They therefore, at first, painted what they wanted to communicate. . . . In time they invented symbolic figures: darts represented war; an eye signified divinity."

In July, 1857, Tolstoy wrote in his diary:

". . . and the most important of all: clearly and forcibly the thought came to me to open a school for the entire county."

Only two years later, in the fall of 1859, he came close to realising his dreams. With the same passion with which he did everything, he gave himself to teaching. Almost to the exclusion of all other interests, he gave three years of his life to the peasant children. His work had nothing in common with the standard, well-regulated school systems. Tolstoy wrote that he had a passionate affection for his school. Under his guidance other young people who helped him in his work developed a similar "passionate affection."

As usual he began by discarding all existing traditions and by refusing to follow any method of teaching already in use. First he must fathom the mind of the peasant child, and by doing away with punishments, let his pupils

26

teach him the art of teaching. In his school his pupils were free to choose their own subjects, and to take as much work as they desired. The teacher considered it his duty to assist the children in their search for knowledge by adjusting his method of approach to the individual child, and by finding the best way of proffering assistance in each case.

These free Tolstoy schools, without programmes, without punishments, without rules, without forcing the will of a child, were remarkably successful. The children spent entire days at their studies and were reluctant to leave the schoolhouse.

Fifty years later, Basil Borosov, one of the peasants, said, "Hours passed like minutes. If life were always as gay no one would ever notice it go by. . . . In our pleasures, in our gaiety, in our rapid progress, we soon became as thick as thieves with the Count. We were unhappy without the Count and the Count was unhappy without us. We were inseparable, and only night drew us apart. . . . There was no end to our conversations. We told him a lot of things; about sorcerers, about forest devils. . . ."

And one of the international volunteers in Kabylia in the mountains of Algeria writes:

"About twenty children were sitting in front of the teacher under an ash tree and reading in chorus the name of their village which she had written on a big sheet of paper. They were enormously proud; time and time again they read us the word.

27

"But the next evening three of the adults came to ask us to teach them to write their names.

" 'Why do you want to write your name?'

"One of them explained: 'To sign at the Post Office. If I can sign my name to collect a registered letter I shall not need to pay the witnesses.'

" 'And do you often get letters like that?'

" 'Sometimes. From my son in France.'

"We went steadily on; but in the evening, instead of resting under the mosquito net, we were all caught up in the fever of fundamental education."

Organic reading for beginners is not new; it's our rejection of it that's new.

The Key Vocabulary

The method of teaching any subject in a Maori infant room may be seen as a plank in a bridge from one culture to another, and to the extent that this bridge is strengthened may a Maori in later life succeed.

This transition made by Maori children is often unsuccessful. At a tender age a wrench occurs from one culture to another, from which, either manifestly or subconsciously, not all recover. And I think that this circumstance has some little bearing on the number of Maoris who, although well educated, seem neurotic, and on the number who retreat to the mat.

Another more obvious cause of the social failure of Maoris is the delay in the infant room. Owing to this delay, which is due to language as well as to the imposition of a culture, many children arrive at the secondary school stage too old to fit in with the European group and they lose heart to continue. From here, being too young and unskilled to do a competent job, some fall in and out of trouble, become failures by European standards, and by the time they have grown up have lost the last and most precious of their inheritances—their social stability.

With this in mind, therefore, I see any subject whatever in a Maori infant room as a plank in the bridge from the Maori to the European. In particular, reading.

So, in preparing reading for a Maori infant room, a teacher tries to bridge the division between the races and to jettison the excess time.

Children have two visions, the inner and the outer. Of the two the inner vision is brighter.

I hear that in other infant rooms widespread illustration is used to introduce the reading vocabulary to a five-year-old, a vocabulary chosen by adult educationists. I use pictures, too, to introduce the reading vocabulary, but they are pictures of the inner vision and the captions are chosen by the children themselves. True, the picture of the outer, adult-chosen pictures can be meaningful and delightful to children; but it is the captions of the mind pictures that have the power and the light. For whereas the illustrations perceived by the outer eye cannot be other than interesting, the illustrations seen by the inner eye are organic, and it is the captioning of these that I call the "Key Vocabulary."

I see the mind of a five-year-old as a volcano with two vents; destructiveness and creativeness. And I see that to the extent that we widen the creative channel, we atrophy the destructive one. And it seems to me that since these words of the key vocabulary are no less than the captions of the dynamic life itself, they course out through the creative channel, making their contribution to the drying up of the destructive vent. From all of which I am constrained to see it as creative reading and to count it among the arts.

First words must mean something to a child.

First words must have intense meaning for a child. They must be part of his being.

How much hangs on the love of reading, the instinctive inclination to hold a book! *Instinctive*. That's what it must be. The reaching out for a book needs to become an organic action, which can happen at this yet formative age. Pleasant words won't do. Respectable words won't do. They must be words organically tied up, organically born from the dynamic life itself. They must be words that are already part of the child's being. "A child," reads a recent publication on the approach of the American books, "can be led to feel that Janet and John are friends." *Can be led to feel*. Why lead him to feel or try to lead him to feel that these strangers are friends? What about the passionate feeling he has already for his own friends? To me it is inorganic to overlook this step. To me it is an offence against art. I see it as an interruption in the natural expansion of life of which Erich Fromm speaks. How would New Zealand children get

on if all their reading material were built from the life of African blacks? It's little enough to ask that a Maori child should begin his reading from a book of his own colour and culture. This is the formative age where habits are born and established. An aversion to the written word is a habit I have seen born under my own eyes in my own infant room on occasion.

It's not beauty to abruptly halt the growth of a young mind and to overlay it with the frame of an imposed culture. There are ways of training and grafting young growth. The true conception of beauty is the shape of organic life and that is the very thing at stake in the transition from one culture to another. If this transition took place at a later age when the security of a person was already established there would not be the same need for care. But in this country it happens that the transition takes place at a tender and vulnerable age, which is the reason why we all try to work delicately.

Back to these first words. To these first books. They must be made out of the stuff of the child itself. I reach a hand into the mind of the child, bring out a handful of the stuff I find there, and use that as our first working material. Whether it is good or bad stuff, violent or placid stuff, coloured or dun. To effect an unbroken beginning.

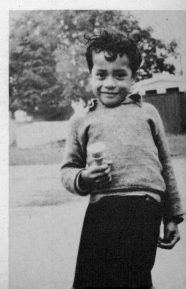

And in this dynamic material, within the familiarity and security of it, the Maori finds that words have intense meaning to him, from which cannot help but arise a love of reading. For it's here, right in this first word, that the love of reading is born, and the longer his reading is organic the stronger it becomes, until by the time he arrives at the books of the new culture, he receives them as another joy rather than as a labour. I know all this because I've done it.

First words must have an intense meaning.
First words must be already part of the dynamic life.
First books must be made of the stuff of the child
himself, whatever and wherever the child.

The words, which I write on large tough cards and give to the children to read, prove to be one-look words if they are accurately enough chosen. And they are plain enough in conversation. It's the conversation that has to be got. However, if it can't be, I find that whatever a child chooses to make in the creative period may quite likely be such a word. But if the vocabulary of a child is still inaccessible, one can always begin him on the general Key Vocabulary, common to any child in any race, a set of words bound up with security that experiments, and later on their creative writing, show to be organically associated with the inner world: "Mummy," "Daddy," "kiss," "frightened," "ghost."

"Mohi," I ask a new five, an undisciplined Maori, "what word do you want?"

"Jet!"

I smile and write it on a strong little card and give it to him. "What is it again?"

"Jet!"

"You can bring it back in the morning. What do you want, Gay?"

Gay is the classic overdisciplined, bullied victim of the respectable mother.

"House," she whispers. So I write that, too, and give it into her eager hand.

"What do you want, Seven?" Seven is a violent Maori.

"Bomb! Bomb! I want bomb!"

So Seven gets his word "bomb" and challenges anyone to take it from him.

And so on through the rest of them. They ask for a new word each morning and never have I to repeat to them what it is. And if you saw the condition of these tough little cards the next morning you'd know why they need to be of tough cardboard or heavy drawing paper rather than thin paper.

When each has the nucleus of a reading vocabulary and I know they are at peace with me I show them the word "frightened" and at once all together they burst out with what they are frightened of. Nearly all the Maoris say "the ghost!" a matter which has a racial and cultural origin, while the Europeans name some animal they have never seen, "tiger" or "alligator," using it symbolically for the unnameable fear that we all have.

"I not frightened of anysing!" shouts my future murderer, Seven.

"Aren't you?"

"No, I stick my knife into it all!"

"What will you stick your knife into?"

"I stick my knife into the tigers!"

"Tigers" is usually a word from the European children but here is a Maori with it. So I give him "tigers" and never have I to repeat this word to him, and in the morning the little card shows the dirt and disrepair of passionate usage.

"Come in," cry the children to a knock at the door, but as no one does come in we all go out. And here we find in the porch, humble with natural dignity, a barefooted, tattooed Maori woman.

"I see my little Seven?" she says.

"Is Seven your little boy?"

"I bring him up. Now he five. I bring him home to his real family for school eh. I see my little boy?"

The children willingly produce Seven, and here we have in the porch, within a ring of sympathetic brown and blue eyes, a reunion.

"Where did you bring him up?" I ask over the many heads.

"Way back on those hill. All by heeself. You remember your ol' Mummy?" she begs Seven.

I see.

Later, standing watching Seven grinding his chalk to dust on his blackboard as usual, I do see. "Whom do you want, Seven? Your old Mummy or your new Mummy?"

"My old Mummy."

"What do your brothers do?"

"They all hits me."

"Old Mummy" and "new Mummy" and "hit" and "brothers" are all one-look words added to his vocabulary, and now and again I see some shape breaking through the chalk-ravage. And I wish I could make a good story of it and say he is no longer violent. . . .

"Who's that crying!" I accuse, lifting my nose like an old war horse.

"Seven he breaking Gay's neck."

So the good story, I say to my junior, must stand by for a while. But I can say he is picking up his words now. Fast.

Dennis is a victim of a respectable, money-making, well-dressed mother who thrashes him, and at five he has already had his first nervous breakdown. "I'm not frightened of anything!" he cries.

"Is Dennis afraid of anything?" I asked his young pretty mother in her big car.

"Dennis? He won't even let the chickens come near him."

"Did you have a dream?" I asked Dennis after his afternoon rest.

"Yes I did."

"Well then . . . where's some chalk and a blackboard?"

Later when I walked that way there was a dreadful brown ghost with purple eyes facing a red alligator on a roadway. I know I have failed with Dennis. I've never had his fear words. His mother has defeated me. During the morning output period—when everyone else is painting, claying, dancing, quarrelling, singing, drawing, talking, writing or building—Dennis is picking up my things from the floor and straightening the mats, and the picture I have of his life waiting for him, another neurotic, pursued by the fear unnameable, is not one of comfort.

Mare resisted any kind of reading vocabulary until

one morning when the Little Ones were all talking at once about what they were frightened of he let go, "I shoot the bulldog!" Gay's fear was a dog too. Do we realise just how afraid small children are of dogs?

But I have some dirty, thoroughly spoilt children next door who are never held up with fear. Their Key Vocabulary runs from "Daddy," and "kiss" through words like "truck," "hill," and "Mummy" to "love" and "train." How glorious are the dirty spoilt children.

Out press these words, grouping themselves in their own wild order. All boys wanting words of locomotion, aeroplane, tractor, jet, and the girls the words of domesticity, house, Mummy, doll. Then the fear words, ghost, tiger, skellington, alligator, bulldog, wild piggy, police. The sex words, kiss, love, touch, *haka*.* The key words carrying their own illustrations in the mind, vivid and powerful pictures which none of us could possibly draw for them—since in the first place we can't see them and in the second because they are so alive with an organic life that the external pictorial representation of them is beyond the frontier of possibility. We can do no more than supply the captions.

Out push these words. The tendency is for them to gather force once the fears are said, but there are so many variations on character. Even more so in this span of life where personality has not yet been moulded into the general New Zealand pattern by the one imposed vocabulary for all. They are more than captions. They are even more than sentences. They are whole stories at times. They are actually schematic drawing. I know because they tell them to me.

Out flow these captions. It's a lovely flowing. I see the creative channel swelling and undulating like an artery with blood pumping through. And as it settles, just like any other organic arrangement of nature it spreads out into an harmonious pattern; the fear words dominating the design, a few sex words, the person interest, and the temper of the century. Daddy, Mummy, ghost, bomb, kiss, brothers, butcher knife, gaol, love, dance, cry, fight, hat, bulldog, touch, wild piggy . . . if you were a child,

* *haka:* Maori war dance.

which vocabulary would you prefer? Your own or the one at present in the New Zealand infant rooms? Come John come, Look John look. Come and look. See the boats? The vocabulary of the English upper middle class, two-dimensional and respectable?

Out pelt these captions, these one-word accounts of the pictures within. Is it art? Is it creation? Is it reading? I know that it is integral. It is organic. And it is the most vital and the most sure reading vocabulary a child can build. It is the key that unlocks the mind and releases the tongue. It is the key that opens the door upon a love of reading. It is the organic foundation of a lifetime of books. It is the key that I use daily with my fives, along with the clay and the paint and amid the singing and quarrelling.

It is the key whose turning preserves intact for a little longer the true personality. It is the Key Vocabulary.

MAXIMS
in the preparation of
Maori Infant Reading

The Key Vocabulary centers round the two main instincts, fear and sex.

The Key Vocabulary varies from one locality to another and from one race to another.

Backward readers have a private Key Vocabulary which once found launches them into reading.

The power content of a word can be determined better from a backward reader than from an average reader.

In the presentation of key words to five-year-olds, illustrations are to be shunned rather than coveted.

The length of a word has no relation to its power content.

In all matters in a Maori infant room there is a Maori standard as well as a European one.

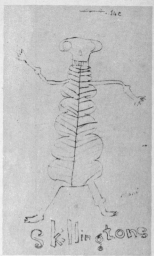

I said earlier that the illustrations chosen by adults to introduce the reading vocabulary could be meaningful and delightful, but that it was the picture of the inner vision and the captions chosen by the children themselves that had the power and the light. However, there is still the odd child who is too emotionally disturbed to caption the inner picture at all.

Rangi, a backward Maori, after learning to recognize eight Maori nouns, stalled on the words "come," "look," "and" for weeks until it occurred to me to ask him what he was frightened of. He said he was frightened of the police. Asked why, he replied that the police would take him to gaol in the fire engine, cut him up with a butcher knife, kill him and hang up what was left of him. When I told the Head about this, he said that Rangi's father ran a gambling den down at the hotel to keep the home going and himself in beer and that the whole family lived in the shadow of the police and that the children had probably been theatened in order not to tell.

When I gave these words to Rangi—police, butcher knife, kill, gaol, hand and fire engine—they proved themselves to be one-look words. Whereas he had spent four months on "come," "look," "and," he spent four minutes on these. So from these I made him reading

cards, and at last Rangi was a reader.

Puki, who comes from a clever family, and whose mother and father fight bitterly and physically and often, breaking out in the night and alarming the children who wake and scream (I've heard all this myself), after learning two words in six months burst into reading on Daddy, Mummy, Puki, fight, yell, hit, crack, frightened, broom.

It is an opportune moment to observe the emotional distance of these private key vocabularies from the opening words of the "Janet and John" book: Janet John come look and see the boats little dog run here down up . . .

There are always these special cases on the handling of which depends the child's start in school. No time is too long spent talking to a child to find out his key words, the key that unlocks himself, for in them is the secret of reading, the realisation that words can have intense meaning. Words having no emotional significance to him, no instinctive meaning, could be an imposition, doing him more harm than not teaching him at all. They may teach him that words mean nothing and that reading is undesirable.

The fact that certain words can be surmounted by the average reader does not prove them. That's the red herring. The weight of a word is proved by the backward reader. And there are many backward Maori readers. And to begin them on such bloodless words as "come," "look," "and" provokes one to experiment.

The Key Vocabulary of a Maori infant room, outside the common vocabulary of fear and sex, changes all the time like anything else alive, but here is the current Key Vocabulary running through the infant room this week, from the newcomers. All Maoris.

Mohi: ghost jet jeep skellington bike aeroplane sausage porridge egg car beer jersey kiss . . .

Joe Joe: King of the Rocket Men Indian Phantom Superman . . .

Gilbert: frog walnut truck King of the Rocket Men jet jeep beer tractor bomb horse . . .

Moreen: Mummy Daddy Tape [dog] lambie *Kuia* kiss . . .

Penny: Daddy Mummy house plane car . . .

Rongo: peanut cake ghost bed kiss socks . . .

Phillip: train boxing truck pea rifle . . .

Phyllis: beer pudding bus darling kiss ghost . . .

The words when I print them on big cards fill them with smiles and excitement.

Words over the past two years, however, from the Maori newcomers group themselves as follows, all one-look words to the particular child:

Fear (the strongest): Mummy Daddy ghost frightened skellington wild piggy police spider dog gaol bull kill butcher knife yell hit crack fight thunder alligator cry . . .

Sex: kiss love haka dance darling together me-and-you sing . . .

Locomotion: jet jeep aeroplane train car truck trailer bus . . .

Others: house school socks frog walnut peanut porridge pictures beer . . .

Emerging from two years of observation, however, are the two most powerful words in the infant-room vocabulary under any circumstances: ghost, kiss, representing in their own way, possibly, the two main instincts. Any child, brown or white, on the first day, remembers these words from one look.

Yet do I include them in a first reading book? There's no end to courage but there is an end to the strength required to swim against the current. For here again is the opening vocabulary of the "Janet and John":

Janet John come look and see the boats little dog run here down up aeroplane my one kitten one two three play jump can go horse ride.

Between these and the Key Vocabulary is there any emotional difference? There is all the difference between something that comes through the creative vent and something that approaches from the outside. Which is the difference between the organic and the inorganic vocabulary.

THE MECHANICS OF TEACHING THE KEY VOCABULARY

I take the Key Vocabulary in the morning output period when the energy is at its highest, since it is a crea-

tive activity, and I believe that the creative activities are more important than anything else. It's where I place all the mediums of creativeness, between nine and ten-thirty.

I take it the minute they come in before they touch any other medium, because I don't like to interrupt them later when they are deep in blocks of clay. Also I want to catch the first freshness.

The preparation is modest enough. A number of cards

at hand, about a foot long and five inches wide, of cheap drawing-paper quality, and a big black crayon. And a cardboard cover a size or two larger than the cards. And their old cards tipped out on the mat.

I call a child to me and ask her what she wants. She may ask for "socks" and I print it large on a card with her name written quickly in the corner for my own use. She watches me print the word and says it as I print, then

I give it to her to take back to the mat and trace the characters with her finger and finally replace it in the cover nearby. I call them one by one until each child has a new word.

These self-chosen words mount up and are kept in a box. Each morning before the children come in I tip the cards out on the mat so that when they run in from assembly they make straight for them to find their own, not without quarrelling and concentration and satisfaction. When they have collected their own they choose a partner and sit together and hear each other, their own and the other's words. All this, of course, takes time and involves noise and movement and personal relations and actual reading, and above all communication, one with another: the vital thing so often cut off in a schoolroom. And it is while they are teaching each other, far more effectively than I could teach them myself, that I call each one to me separately to get his new word for the day.

The girl who said "socks," perhaps, comes to me with her old words and says them as she puts them back in the box; but the ones she doesn't remember I take from her and destroy because the word has failed as a one-look word and cannot have been of much importance to her. And it is the words that are important to her that I am after. For it is from these words that she first realizes that reading can be of intense meaning to herself. So the only words she keeps are those that have come from deep within herself and have to be told only once.

It is at this stage that I say, "What are you going to have?" Sometimes she will have it all bubbling hot, "Toast!" and sometimes she will twist her foot and think, and then I suspect the validity of it when she looks about and says, "Windows." And as often as not, later in the day when these words are checked she won't recognize it. So I engage her in conversation until I find out that she sleeps with Maude, or that Daddy has gone to the shearing shed. And I ask her again and may get "shed" or "Maude," which might well prove valid. But they're not often like this and I print the asked-for word on the card while she watches me and says it while I print. Then I give it to her to take back to the mat and trace it with her finger before putting it back in the cover.

I make mistakes over the choice of these words on occasion. It take me a little while to assess the character of each newcomer. For the variety of character on the five-year-old level is as legion as nature itself. And there are pitfalls like copying, mood, repression and crippling fears which block the organic expulsion of a word. But you get to know all these after a while and there comes in time, sometimes at once and sometimes later on, a regular flow of organic words which are captions to the pictures in the mind.

It may sound hard, but it's the easiest way I have ever begun reading. There's no driving to it. I don't teach at all. There is no work to put up on the blackboard, no charts to make and no force to marshal the children into a teachable and attentive group. The teaching is done among themselves, mixed up with all the natural concomitants of relationship. I just make sure of my cards nearby and my big black crayon and look forward to the game with myself of seeing how nearly I hit the mark. And the revelation of character is a thing that no one can ever find boring.

After the morning interval, during what I call my intake period the new words of the morning come out of the cover and I check to see which are remembered. They mostly are, but the ones that are not are taken away and old ones take their place, so that when the children attempt to write them they are writing words that carry with them an inner picture and are of organic origin.

Then the words go back in the box to be tipped out on the mat the next morning. When there is a small group of beginners, the number of known words mounting up in the box need have no limit, but in direct ratio to the growing size of the group the number of words kept per child diminishes until with a group of twelve to twenty it is not feasible to keep more than the last few for each child.

NOTES

A minimum of forty personal words before passing on into the next group. But promotion with me depends not on the amount of intake but the rate of intake.

If a child copies a word of another, he won't remember it the next time he meets it.

A new word every week, however shy or speechless or dull the newcomer. In time he will see that the differing marks on this paper mean important different things.

What I call teaching each other: One holds up the card with "socks" to the other and says: "What's that?" If the other doesn't know, the first one tells him.

Organic Writing

"Life as a whole is too complicated to teach to children. The minute it is cut up they can understand it, but you are liable to kill it in cutting it up."
—*C. E. Beeby*

After the Key Vocabulary first thing in the morning they go on to other mediums of expression.

Creative writing follows on from the Key Vocabulary. Whereas the Key Vocabulary is a one-word caption of the inner world, creative writing is a sentence-length or story-length caption. From schematic writing they progress towards the representational.

The creative writing of fives begins with their attempt to write their own key words, and since they have found out that these scrawly shapes mean something, they know what they are writing about more than I do.

From here they join in with the stream of autobiographical writing that they all do in the morning output period, and a few days of this is enough to show any writer or teacher where style begins. Fives have a most distinctive style. And they write these sentences of the same pattern with its varied content so often that they learn automatically the repeated words and consolidate this style. With scarcely any teaching from me, which transfers the whole question of spelling, word study and composition into the vent of creativity.

This self-chosen vocabulary remains with them as they

I got drowned.

Nanny's in the coffin under the ground

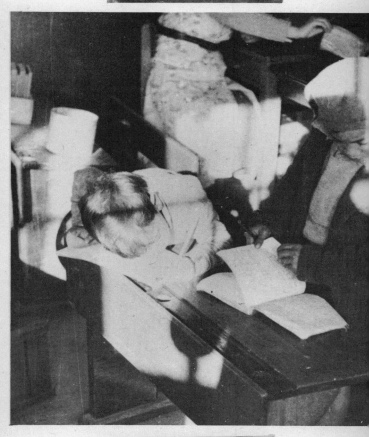

Mummie got a hiding off Daddy He was drunk. she was crying

I went to the river and
I kissed Lily and I ran
away. Then I kissed
Philliga Then I ran away
and went for a swim

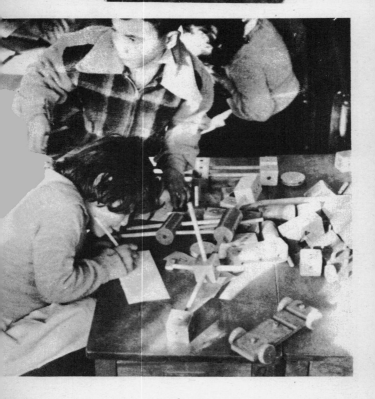

Our baby is dead.
She was dead on
Monday night. When
mummie got it

rise through the infant room, since in the first place these words were part of the mind before they were written at all and in the second place there is a natural repetition. And from them grows a selection of individual vocabularies entered in the back of their writing books where they can be referred to and exchanged. And the standard of spelling which arises from this seems to serve their purpose.

Also there is a general vocabulary springing from their writing which becomes to some modest extent known to most of them sooner or later. Then, and, put, went, cowboy, truck, I, inside, outside, pictures, lollies, the, to, on, place, told, me, Daddy, Mummy, because . . .

After a while, as their capacity increases, they write two sentences about themselves and their lives, then three, until six-year-olds are writing half a page and seven-year-olds a page or more a day. But I don't call it teaching: I call it creativity since it all comes from them and nothing from me, and because the spelling and composition are no longer separate subjects to be taught but emerge naturally as another medium.

The drama of these writings could never be captured in a bought book. It could never be achieved in the most faithfully prepared reading books. No one book could ever hold the variety of subject that appears collectively in the infant room each morning. Moreover, it is written in the language that they use themselves. These books they write are the most dramatic and pathetic and colourful things I've ever seen on pages.

But they are private and they are confidences and we don't criticise their content. Whether we read that he hates school or that my house is to be burned down or about the brawl in the *pa** last night the issue is the same: it is always not what is said but the freedom to say.

I never teach a child something and then get him to write about it. It would be an imposition in the way that it is in art. A child's writing is his own affair and is an exercise in integration which makes for better work. The more it means to him the more value it is to him. And it means everything to him. It is part of him as an arranged

* *pa:* Maori village.

subject could never be. It is not a page of sentences written round set words, resulting in a jumble of disconnected facts as you so often see. It is the unbroken line of thought that we cultivate so carefully in our own writing and conversation.

Since writing of this kind is the most exhaustive of all the mediums used in the output period, I time it early in the morning. Often we break the writing time with expressive dancing since dancing is body-talk anyway. I know for sure that some welcome it, and it may help composition, but I don't know.

The whole exercise of creative writing, the reaching back into the mind for something to say, nurtures the organic idea and exercises the inner eye; and it is this calling on the child's own resources that preserves and protracts a little longer his own true personality.

THE MECHANICS OF TEACHING ORGANIC WRITING

Ten o'clock is backache time. By then you have spent an half hour bending over the children writing at their low desks. But there's no alternative. Not only do you enter the words they ask for at the back of their books, but, bearing in mind the reading of them afterwards,

you watch the spacing of the words for better legibility, carefully oversee the grammar and, above all, nurture the continuity of their thought. You correct as they go along, not after.

It's no good sitting at the table and letting the children queue up. You've got to be mobile and available to all. You've got to exercise something like an all-seeing eye all the time and all at once, which makes me think that this period of organic writing drains even more from a teacher than an art period. So that the backache of giving equals to the backache of bending.

Twelve is the uttermost limit for one teacher. Eight is about the proper number. I take them when the rest of the room is self-dependent in the development period. The noise doesn't matter. The children writing are just about as talkative as the others. But I let it be like that. Suppression is the last thing in organic work.

When I had a junior assistant we both got to work. But when I didn't, I would have two senior boys enter the words, a week's worth at a time, while I watched the spacing, the grammar and the line of thought. Maybe some people never knew there was a line of thought in an infant.

But this work soon shows that there is. One of the hazards met in organic writing is the conversation between them, during which a child tells his neighbor all that he wants to say, so that he skips the necessity of putting it down and writes something like "Then I went home," which closes the subject irrevocably. Against this, however, I don't allow them to write "Then I went home" at all. Giving no reason. So that when they start off, "I went to the pa," the next sequence is what happened at the pa. And once you've got them over that hazard, the line of thought takes care of itself. But it's not a usual risk.

I used to think that a statement of theirs must be finished at all costs at the one sitting; but it turns out that you can close down safely at a definite time, because they can pick up what they were writing the day before with no trouble at all. They just read it over and go on. Although, for all that, the half-hour often extends. It depends on how well or otherwise you are covering the work, which in turn depends on how many you have writing.

With my children there is no occasion to start them off formally. Having been bred on the Key Vocabulary and through the two-word and three-word sentences, they start naturally enough. Sometimes I still say "What are you going to say?" but the need becomes increasingly rare. If, however, one is really stuck, you do what you have done all along: engage him in conversation, and in no time there is the thing off his mind.

Yet there are times when one cannot start. He's just

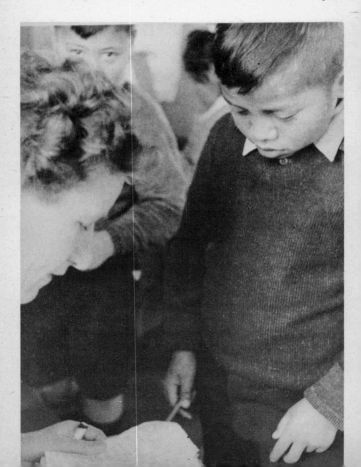

plain not in the mood. You can't always say an important thing because it is the time to say it. Sometimes he will say candidly, "I don't want to write," and that's just what you get him to write: "I don't want to write." From there you ask, "Why?" and here comes an account of some grievance or objection which, after all, just as well as any other idea, delivers his mind of what is on it, practises his composition, and wraps him up in what is of interest to himself.

You never want to say that it's good or bad. That's got nothing to do with it. You've got no right at all to criticise the content of another's mind. A child doesn't make his own mind. It's just there. Your job is to see what's in it. Your only allowable comment is one of natural interest in what he is writing. As in conversation. And I never mark their books in any way; never cross out anything beyond helping them to rub out a mistake, never put a tick or a stamp on it and never complain of bad writing. Do we complain of a friend's writing in a strongly-felt letter? The attention is on the content.

What I feel about their work has nothing to do with it. The thing is for them to write what is on their minds and if they do or do not accomplish that, it is you who are good or bad. From the teacher's end it boils down to whether or not she is a good conversationalist; whether or not she has the gift or the wisdom to listen to another; the ability to draw out and preserve that other's line of thought. Which refers to the nature of the teacher. The best juniors I had on this work were the modest, self-effacing kind, while the worst of them was a very clever girl who was an insatiable talker and who in her personal life talked everyone else to pieces on the subject of herself. And in that year I had the lowest level of organic writing on record.

Ten o'clock is backache time. But did any fruitful effort ever not bend us? "The labour we long for physics pain."

Organic Reading

*"A child comes up, if at all, in accordance with
the law of his own growth."*

—Dr. Burrow

It's a sad thing to say of the vocabulary of any set
reading books for an infant room that it must necessarily
be a dead vocabulary. Yet I say it. For although the first
quality of life is change, these vocabularies never change.
Winter and summer, for brown race or white, through
loud mood or quiet, the next group of words, related
or not to the current temper of the room, inexorably moves
into place for the day's study.

I tried to meet this division between the climate of a
room and an imposed reading book by making another
set of books from the immediate material, but all I did
was to compose another dead vocabulary. For although
they are closer to the Maori children than the books of
the English upper-middle class, their vocabulary is static
too, and it is not the answer to the question I have asked
myself for years: What is the organic reading vocabulary?

At last I know: Primer children write their own books.

Early in the morning this infant room gets under way
on organic writing, and it is this writing that I use in
relative proportions as the reading for the day; for the
children just off the Key Vocabulary with their stories of
two words up to those who can toss off a page or so. In
this way we have a set of graded brand-new stories every
morning, each sprung from the circumstances of their
own lives and illustrated unmatchably in the mind.

The new words they have asked for during the morn-

ing's writing, and which have been entered in the back of their books, they put up on the blackboard each morning. The words range from one or two to ten or so. They reconsider these words after the morning interval when they come in for the intake hour. They read them and spell them for ten minutes. I don't require that they should all be learned and remembered. If they are important enough they will stay, all right, whatever the length. Neither is it for me to sort out which is important. I never say, "Spell 'pictures.' " I say, "Perri, spell one of your words." Then I get the real word and the right spelling. In fact, this is a thing that I hand to them: hearing each other spell. Sometimes, however, we run over these words before dispersing for lunch, and what they have picked up from the morning's writing and reading of the organic work, in terms of numbers of new words and their varying difficulties is sometimes a surprise.

Each afternoon, however, all the words, whether known or not, are rubbed from the board and each morning the new ones go up. It's exciting for us all. No one ever knows what's coming. Wonderful words appear: helicopter, lady's place, cowboy, sore ear, fish and chips, dirt, Captain Marble, mumps, Superman and King of the Rocket Men. Words following intimately from day to day the classroom mood; echoing the *tangi** in the district, recounting the pictures in the hall the night before or

* *tangi:* Maori funeral.   55

revealing the drama behind the closed doors of the pa.

This is the main reading of the day. They master their own story first, then tackle someone else's. There is opportunity to read out their own story and it is from this reading that discussions arise. And since every background of every story is well known to all, the inner illustration flashes very brightly and the discussions are seldom sluggish.

In reading one another's stories, reference is continually made to the writer for the identification of new words. This hardly hurts the writer. Unwittingly, energetically and independently of me, they widen the intake.

How much easier and more pleasant all this is when the stories are followed with a personal interest, and with the whole of the background seen alive in the mind. The facts of suitable printing, length of line and intelligibility run nowhere in the race with meaning. As for word recurrence, there occurs a far more natural one here than anything we could work out. A word recurs as long as they want it and is then dropped cold: a word is picked

up like a new friend and dropped when it becomes boring. Which is what I mean when I say it is a live vocabulary. Things happen in it.

Since I take this original writing as a basis for reading, a strict watch is kept on grammar and punctuation. And as for the writing itself, the handwriting I mean, it has to be at least the best that they can do, to save their own faces, when changing books. Which brings one more subject into the vent of creativity: handwriting.

This organic reading, however, is not meant to stand alone: it is essentially a lead up and out to all the other reading, and as a child rises through the infant room, reaching further and further out to the inorganic and standard reading, there is a comfortable movement from the inner man outward, from the known to the unknown, from the organic to the inorganic. The thing is to keep it a gracious movement, for it is to the extent that the activity in an infant room is creative that the growth of mind is good.

THE MECHANICS OF TEACHING ORGANIC SPELLING

After play, at eleven during the intake period, we turn our attention to the new words themselves. The children pick up their books and run to the blackboard and write them up: the words asked for during the writing of the morning. They're not too long ago to be forgotten. Some of them are, when a child has asked a lot, but they ask you what they are.

Since they are all on the wall blackboard, I can see them from one position. They write them, revise them, the older children spell them and the younger merely say them, but each child is at his own individual level and working to his own particular capacity. Some of them read the word to me—if the group is too big for them all to get round the blackboard—but they all hear each other. You obtain this necessary "you and me" again. Of course, there is a lot of noise, but there's a lot of work too.

Sometimes I say, "Who can spell a word?" and I am given from those who can a word that is instinctively within their compass and which, in any case, is a word of meaning to the child himself. He wants to spell it. More-

over, attached to this word is an unaided inner illustration. Spelling evolves easily and cheerfully. True, hard words are abandoned on occasion, according to the relation of the age of the child to the challenge of the word, but often they are industriously learned owing to their emotional value. Words the size of "sky rocket" get themselves spelled from no drive of mine; "skeleton," "lollies" and so on; while few boys do not know how to spell "cowboy." It's not a hard period for the teacher, this one. Taking in seems to be easier than putting out. Besides, the latent energy, the element that so severely opposes a teacher when imposing knowledge, is here turned on what they are doing. It's an energy that is almost frightening when released. True, there is noise to it that some would object to as unprofessional; but when did I ever claim to be professional?

The writing up and spelling of these words take about a quarter of an hour and from here the children run with their books to the ring of small chairs prepared beforehand for the reading and exchange.

THE MECHANICS OF TEACHING ORGANIC READING

About a quarter of an hour for the reading.

You can tell by the state of these books they write daily whether or not the organic reading is going ahead.

Contrary to the look of a room, they should end up in tatters. When a teacher handed me a group of books recently in irreproachable condition, I knew that the largest point of the whole organic pattern had been overlooked: the reading of and the discussion of one another's books. All art is communication. We never really make things for ourselves alone. The books are to be read to another.

When I had a junior, she took time off to keep abreast of the mending of these books, and when I didn't have one, I made my morning rounds armed with a roll of Cellotape as well as a pencil, rubber and razor blade and mended as I went. It was hard at first to pass these dilapidated books to an inspector, but I got over it. Once I had some exercise books made at the press, of light drawing paper, with a view to precluding the wear and tear, but although they cost considerably more they tore just the same. The drawing paper should have been of heavier weight. But economy comes into this. However, I have not yet worked out what would be the easier on the committee funds: the outlay on cellotape or on drawing paper. One young teacher practising the organic work told me that she couldn't go on with it until she had mended her books, little realising that from her confession I knew that the work was being thoroughly done.

Sitting in their ring of chairs, the childern read again their own and then each other's. I regularly invite them to read aloud to the others. But there's got to be a very light hand or the discussion will not follow. And this discussion is the most significant of all. It is the climax of the whole organic purpose. When we are engaged on this, I arrange that the smaller children are outside for games or story with a junior assistant or a senior pupil. For the organic writing itself proves to be a startling point of departure into talk that would not occur otherwise. It leads into revelations that range from the entertaining to the outrageous. But, beyond a normal show of interest, you don't comment. You neither praise nor blame; you observe. You let everything come out, uncensured; otherwise, why do it at all?

About a quarter of an hour for the reading, taking you to half past eleven, then about a quarter of an hour on discussion, on what I call "talk." It may seem a long time for talk in school, but the very least I can say is that I gain knowledge of my material, and the most I can say is that I could never see anything retarding in the "passionate interchange of talk."

The last quarter of the hour from eleven to twelve they read Maori infant readers. It's all intake. I'm not ashamed of eleven till twelve.

Maori Transitional Readers

The Key Vocabulary and the creative writing have shown me into every corner of a Maori five-year-old mind. I feel I know it inside out. I've got books and books written by these small brown people on the subject of themselves. Sentence-length and story-length captions of the pictures within. Not that their writings are the only evidence. Working with them every day as we do we learn their moods, their tragedies and their desires whether we wish to or not.

From this soil the Maori Transitional Readers have grown. And I mean exactly that: grown. Six years of experiment and a hundred other books precede these final four. Many are the times I have put a book with the paint still wet into a Maori hand and watched for the reaction. And on many an occasion I have found myself in a blind alley.

It was the *temperament* of the pa that had to be got into these books. The instinctive living, the drama, the communal sympathy and the violence. Life in the pa is so often a sequence of tears, tenderness, brawls, beer, love and song. I know because I have been part of it all. In the pa tears still hold the beauty and the importance that the European has long since disclaimed.

Why is sorrow in such disgrace in infant-room reading fare? Where are the wonderful words "kiss" and "cry"? The exciting words "ghost" and "darling"? Everyday words in European homes as well as Maori ones. Kingsley's water-baby, Tom, had his despair, Alice in Wonderland found herself in tight corners, and David Copperfield had occasion enough to weep. Why then is the large part of infant-room reading so carefully and placidly two-dimensional? Is there any time of life when tears and trouble are not a part of living? I think sometimes of the children in the slums faced with these happy smooth books, and feel the same about them as I do about Maori primers. Do the word experts who assemble these books assume that by putting peaceful books into the hands of children they will be an influence for peaceful living? When I see children turning from the respectable, rhythmless stories that parents think it wisest to give them to the drama and violence of comics I think it might be the other way.

Sometimes I relax the children with eyes closed to dream. When they awake I hear these dreams. The violence of those has to be heard to be believed. A lot of it

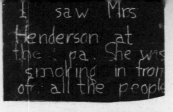

I saw Mrs Henderson at the pa. She was smoking in front of all the people.

I don't like Mrs Henderson She wears black.

I love Mrs Henderon best in the world

is violence against me—which they tell me cheerfully enough. I come out very badly. My house has been burnt down, bombs fall on me, I'm shot with all makes of guns and handed over to the gorilla. Presumably it's the authority and discipline which I represent.

The distance between the content of their minds, however, and the content of our reading books is nothing less than frightening. I can't believe that Janet and John never fall down and scratch a knee and run crying to Mummy. I don't know why their mother never kisses them or calls them "darling." Doesn't John ever disobey? Has the American child no fears? Does it never rain or blow in America? Why is it always fine in primer books? If these questions are naïve it must be because of the five-year-old company I keep. Heaven knows we have enough lively incident in our Maori infant rooms. The fights, the loveships, and the uppercuts from the newcomers. I see the respectable happy reading book placed like a lid upon all this—ignoring, hiding and suppressing it.

Into the text and pictures of these transitional books I have let a little of the drama through. A few of the tears. A good bit of the fears, some of the love, and an implication of the culture. From the rich soil of the Key Vocabulary and the creative writing I can do no less. Even if I did deplore dramatic living, which I don't. To me it is life complete with its third dimension and since Beethoven and Tchaikovsky see it the same way, I am this time in more august company.

Nevertheless I gladly acknowledge the place of the "Janet and John" books in a Maori infant room. But their presence there is not the issue. The issue is simply the transition of a Maori at a tender and vulnerable age from one culture to another, from the pa to the European education.

A five, meeting words for the first time and finding that they have intense meaning for him, at once loves reading. And this is the second issue. Love of reading. Love of a book. When I have observed my Maori fives stalling on the opening "Janet and John," I have seen in my mind simultaneously the lifetime of comic-book reading to follow and the delinquency beyond. However good a book is it can't supply the transitional needs unless it is in sympathy with the Maori children, has incident which they understand and temperament which they sense. Only in a familiar atmosphere can reading be evolutionary, in much the same way as the Key Vocabulary is organic, and it is to supply these needs that the pa or Transitional Books have been composed.

Since their purpose is to bridge a gap (a gap of two thousand years between the races) rather than to teach English, I use the pa vernacular as an overlap.

The word "eh?" so heavily used in Maori speech is a carry-over from the Maori language, from *nei?* used constantly in Maori chat at the end of a sentence, the equivalent to our "Isn't it?" "Don't we?" "Haven't they?" "Don't you think?" and like phrases. Maori children begin sentences with it sometimes: "Eh, Mrs. H.? We're going to the river, eh?" It's one of the necessities in the text of a Maori Transition Book. And to hear Maori children read these sentences with "eh?" is reward enough for the expenditure of courage in writing it. "We play, eh?" "Me and you, eh?" "You stay by me, eh, Daddy?" A sound for sore ears. Where has droning got to? Get them to read "Let us play. They are at home. Mother is in the house."

I see in a current supplementary for primers the conversation of Quacky the Duck.

"I do not like the pond. I do not want to live here."

Has the compiler never heard of the word "don't"? Who in heaven—or in hell, for that matter—speaks like this? *Cadence!* Has no one heard of the word? Does no one read poetry? Why must reading be made harder for fives by the outlawing of cadence? I do not know, I do not know, I do not, I do not.

I don't delay the delivery of a thought by saying "He is not naughty," but say "He's not naughty." "Where's Ihaka?" "He'll get a hiding." "Kuri's at home." "Pussy's frightened." "I'll come back." In grown-up novels we enjoy the true conversational medium, yet five-year-olds for some inscrutable reason are met with the twisted idea behind "Let us play." As a matter of fact, Maoris seldom if ever use "let" in that particular setting. They say "We play, eh?"

These allowances of the natural dialogue preserve cadence and are no harder to learn than any other words. A little easier possibly since cadence is the natural outcome of the running conversational style, the style that is integral. Which brings me back to the consideration of reading books as an integral factor in a child's life.

In word recurrence, sentence length and page length I have only open admiration for the American work. And I follow it respectfully and slavishly in the Maori books. The framework, like so much else that is American, is so good. It's only the content that is slightly respectable for Maoris and me.

How the schematic level of illustration came about is more a matter of evolution than of reason. A matter of instinct maybe. A matter of revulsion possibly' against respectability and the "right thing" that Maoris and I find so intimidating. I can illustrate on the representational level but I like the schematic. And another thing I have found out in this byway of art is that a schematic drawing can convey much emotion. I have illustrated delicate adult poetry this way. And Maori infants in all their candour have never yet challenged this frivolity. Maybe schematic drawing is a language of their own that they reciprocally understand. I have some books at school illustrated by the children themselves. Fascinating, to make an absurd understatement. Anyway an illustrator can hardly help his style, and it's the children who are the judges. I feel that when I come down to their level in text it's a matter of harmony to come back to their level in drawing too. At its worst it honours their own medium, and is the converse of the adult who laughs at children's efforts. And at its best it's a tongue with which to say what I want to.

Speed has pressed this style into curves. There's no time to attend to straight lines when illustrating stories on the blackboard as you tell them or picturing books in a hurry. However, so far there has been no accusation from my judges.

I know hardly anything about colour, but after illustrating dozens of books the urgency of the pace has pressed out, like the curved lines, a simple formula. I should be ashamed to fall so far out of step with my five-year-olds as to see a tree as green and a sky as blue. In the Maori infant rooms over the years I have been brought up amid black roofs, orange houses, green ears, yellow faces, purple trucks and turquoise rain, so if I am charged with riot in colour it's the company I keep. How they draw I draw and what they write I write.

In the familiar setting of the Maori Transitional Books a Maori child may accomplish the mechanics of reading, simultaneously realising that reading means something personal. At this preliminary stage he has a chance to believe in reading and from his experience he can carry within him a confidence to any other reading book; with or without the natural dialogue, with or without the third dimension, with or without the pa temperament and with or without turquoise rain. He is equipped with a little reading ability and a measure of confidence, and under these conditions the "Janet and John" books can be a step of delight.

All of which brings me to another thought. It is possible that the transitional reading, easing as it does the whole reading process, may have some bearing on the length of time a Maori spends in an infant room, given good attendance. Those of my children who attend regularly do make it in two years but I'm wary of spectacular results in experiment. So do some other Maoris in other infant rooms clear the primers in two years. Transitional reading however could help to forestall the situation arising at the top of a school: the familiar picture of four-teens and fifteens too old to go to high school, too young and untrained to do a skilled job, holding an authentic grudge against European education and ripe for delin-quency. Even if this preliminary conditioning of the tran-sitional reading helped to take even one year off the Standard 6 age it would not be wholly futile.

How important is this early approach to reading? Can it be, in any unseen way, related to many a Maori's aver-sion to reading anything beyond comics in later life? Pos-sibly not. I think that's a matter of racial development.

The Maori Transitional Books are used not as a substi-tute for the American books but as a lead up to them. They condition a Maori child to be able to use the "Janet and John" series more wholly. They have been designed to help bridge the breach between the races and are a modest contribution towards the preservation of a Ma-ori's social stability in later life. I know they differ from the current literature of an infant room on some contro-versial issues, but so are Maoris different from us. The thing that is so constantly forgotten by the majority race in judging Maori life is that there is a Maori standard as well as an European one.

Nevertheless it is to the standard of Maori five-year-olds that I have measured these books.

The Golden Section

"Many centuries ago Plato and Pythagoras had already found in *number* the clue to the *nature* of the universe and to the mystery of beauty."

But in school it works out to be of more practical importance to realise these two aspects, nature study and number, as differences, rather than as the fundamental unity that they are, even though number has never been anything other than the basis of all forms which nature assumes.

However, the more a subject refers to its source, the more chance it has of being integrated, and although nature study and number are indispensable landmarks in a syllabus, their separation reminds me of the "cutting up

67

of life," to which Mr. Beeby refers; also I wonder if Tolstoy would have done it this way. I personally see it easier to subordinate them both to a title which has in it the meaning of both. And although there are other deeply rooted points from which nature study and number arise as a unity, there is one which has a particular relation to plant growth: the Golden Section.

The Golden Section is the ideal proportion. It is the division of a distance in such a way that the shorter part is to the longer part as the longer part is to the whole. It's one of the laws governing plant life, and although it is something that cannot be explained in an infant room, it can be felt all right and it can be drawn easily and every day. The diminishing spans between twigs on a branch as it tapers to its tip. Or on a fern. Ferns make wonderful counting boards. When we were on long trips when our children were little, we would sometimes give them a big frond to count, and as an occupational toy I can recommend it. Costs nothing. Just pick one from the side of the road. And all the time they were learning fundamental things about natural form.

However, to return to the infant room, all this going outside ("outside," by the way, has turned out to be a pathetically strong word in the Organic Vocabulary)—all this going outside to see and handle these things and the returning to draw and write about them is the way to find out about this section. The laws of number, nature and beauty turn out to be much the same thing.

Yet there is no evidence to suspect the validity of much of the number material available to an infant room; for instance the square things and the many pieces that are built on even numbers; but the idea has its duplicate often enough outdoors—in the right-angled leafing arrangements and the pairs of leaves set exactly opposite each other as in the koromiko. Some of the infant-room material has gradations, too; not quite the two-three-five-eight-thirteen combination of the tapering nodules of plants but gradations anyway. It's an idea to write this sequence on the blackboard for bead-threading purposes, as a variation to the even sets of two, then of three and so on. It's more exciting, seeing the size of the bead group growing along the string. But the most absorbing number activity is the drawing of a fern frond by the children; ten on this twig, nine on this, eight on this until the one on its own at the end; numbering them.

Then sometimes in the lower groups you can draw a hand, tracing your own hand on the paper and numbering the fingers, when learning to count to five. Or toes. Or a flower with its petals, real flowers outside, unpicked. They make good sums for upper primers, flowers. And it can all happen in a walk and there's nothing destroyed. And there are scents to go with it and beauty.

Clover is an incomparable activity in threes and it's just out the door. Also it is something you can pick in quantities and bring inside. For upper primers learning to count in threes and for the Little Ones learning to count to three. But counting the impermanent birds is the most concentrated game, involving a self-imposed quiet and watchful eyes, and there's the drawing or painting or clay record to follow.

Things don't always work out as ideally as that though. When it's raining or cold we turn to material and chalk. But on a fine morning we all go for a walk down the stop-bank. We play games in it and some of the girls dance the "Babes in the Wood" ballet and cover two children with leaves. We note the turning colour all around and use the word "autumn."

We count the children we can see and work out the ones that are missing. The boy who is sent back to school for disobedience makes a subtraction sum, and the strays we pick up on our way, the half-past fours, addition. The last time we went we each took a small branch and counted the leaves on it. They ranged from six to seventeen. Then I told the children to count a hundred trees in the willow plantation, touching each tree, and afterwards we went on down to the sand by the river and wrote our numbers with sticks.

The thing about all this is that they like doing it and become easy to teach. But they just as much like the games and weighing and snakes and ladders and dominoes and skittles for the winter. And the seven-year-olds try some formal sums and try to write up to a hundred. There's even a place for how many pennies in a shilling, although maybe that belongs beyond what I

call the plastic age of children. At this time, when a mind is setting into its permanent future pattern, it might just as well set into a pattern akin to nature. There's time enough for formality and respectability afterwards. So we go for long, noisy, happy walks along the stop-bank by the river. All sorts of things can happen in a walk, not the least being experience itself. To write about or talk or draw about. Then the Golden Section becomes inseparable from writing and reading and drawing and conversation. Three ducks on the wing we like better than three ducks on a number card with a static three beside them.

I think that we don't like seeds grown in eggshells and nasturtiums and onions in tins and a bulb in a jar in the classroom. We like eggs in eggshells, jam in tins, bulbs in the garden and nasturtiums by the fence. When we want to see the construction of a seedling there are mil-

lions outside. I hate charts as much as they do. I like the moving currents of children's interests. Draw the poplars straight after a walk and count them and number them. Then drop the subject for the next. I like the "hot prison of the moment."

We don't waste enough in school. We hoard our old ideas on charts to be used again and again like stale bread. Ideas are never the same again, even those of the masters; even if the only change is in our own mood of reapproach. Yet there's never a shortage of ideas if the stimulus is there. Waste the old paper and waste the old pictures and waste the old ideas. It's tidier and simpler.

Birds in our area: Sparrows, mynah, crow, magpie, thrush, blackbird, fantail, fowls, duck, geese.

Unwilling insects brought into school: Mantis, grasshoppers, caterpillars, beetles, crickets, butterflies.

Uninvited insects in school: Wasps, lice, bees, spiders.

71

One early autumn we had the monarch butterfly cater-pillars on the swan plant and watched or tried to watch the sequences of their development into butterflies, but owing to the help given by some of my Maori warriors the butterflies never made it. Over in the junior room, however, they managed to get through.

I think there may be a lack of sympathy between the infant room and the insect world since the enrollment of the wasps. Last week as Arapata was on his way across the playground to get his typhoid injection, a wasp gave him one instead. He got to the nurse all right but not with the same intention. No one pressed him to receive the needle. Not that morning anyway. And when I put Joe outside the other day for discipline's sake, screams told us that the wasps had completed the discipline, so we brought him inside again. We've had no trouble with him since. All of which has provoked passionate discus-sions on wasps and their ways. Also some passionate paintings.

The birds have supplied us with movements for expres-sive dancing. There's a magpie dance and a lark dance, although we have seen no larks. We've been told that there are larks, however, but not the spectacular high-flying, high-singing ones. The falling leaves supply us with endless dance designs, both formal and informal. Also the fin movement of fish. And frogs. We've had some frogs inside in tins of muddy, grassy water for ob-servation, but once more the loving ways of my warriors bring their lives to an early close. Also the frogs of these parts are great jumpers and for some reason prefer the machine drawer or the coal tin to the cool water. Or get themselves mixed up in the clay bucket or go for the books. Sammy Snail is the only visitor who has the sense to keep out of reach, dangling on the rafter. And we have a chrysalis or two. Pussy doesn't get much of a time when she strolls in and I don't think the ginger rooster will ever call again.

Informal visitors to the infant room: Sammy Snail, Ginger Rooster, Pussy, Mangu's dog, a fantail, a monkey.

We had some goldfish to watch for a time. They were kept in the senior room and were a great draw to the infants. But owing to the container leaking they were put in the tub in the laundry to ensure the automatic replacement of water. But one laundry day some soap fell in . . . Amen.

I have gathered over the years a collection of pictures, however, of different subjects, some of them animals, some of them birds, along with the nursery rhymes and seasonal pictures, and mounted them, and I keep them in separate packets. Wet day stuff. And they greatly widen the horizon. There's a packet of about thirty pictures of bears, for instance, to follow up on the Three Bears story. Autumn pictures, horse pictures, bird pictures and cat pictures. But they are used for the observation of nature only when we are short of the real live thing, kicking, crawling, singing or stinging.

I place the Golden Section in the output period between one o'clock and two—either for the whole of the time, as during a walk, or for a number lesson outside to be written about when they come in, or for part of the time. So much depends on mood and weather and attendance. The pictures, though, occur in the intake period between eleven and twelve.

The formal number scheme which is provided for our use is essentially creative and belongs in the morning.

Also one soon collects seasonal songs and poems and stories about animals and birds and weather, *e.g.:*

SPRING

Songs: Buttercups and Daisies; Hark, Hark, the Lark; The North Wind.
Poems: Chick-chick; Violet; Jonquil.
Stories: The Black Cat; The Apple-blossom.

SUMMER

Songs: The Birds in the Trees; Catching Fishes.
Poems: Kees-kees; Lady-bird.
Stories: Miscellaneous; Little Red Hen.

AUTUMN

Songs: The Falling Leaves; Rustle, Rustle; A Little Brown Baby.
Poem: Ten Little Yellow Leaves.
Stories: Miscellaneous; "Janet and John" stories.

Songs: The South Wind; Jolly Little Eskimo; Mr. Wind; Pitter-Patter; The Rain Fairy.

Poems: Children, Children; Jack Frost.

Story: The Three Goats.

Flowers in our area: Marigolds, stock, roses, poppies, currants, pansies, geraniums, dahlias, dephiniums.

Trees in our area: Cabbage trees, macrocarpa, hoheria, walnut, most fruit trees, pine.

Experience and record could well be the story of the Golden Section. There can't be any tight compartments of age or time or work coverage. I think that this tracking down of number and nature study to their deep common source may give back in integration what it takes from the expertly planned lesson. At least as much. And I think that if we take care of the Golden Section, its parts, nature study and number, will, in the infant room anyway, take care of themselves.

Tone

"The still centre"
—*T. S. Eliot*

Tone belongs to order and can be won.

It concerns not only classrooms; it is a condition that is or is not implicit in every group of people working together over something, from infant rooms through education departments to groups as big as countries. For in the running of all these, order is the key. It's the expression on the countenance of a group.

But there are two kinds of order, and which is the one we wish for: Is it the conscious order that ends up as respectability? Or is it the unconscious order that looks like chaos on the top? There is a separate world on each side of this question mark.

When we track tone to its source we find that it inhabits the temperament area. We find that the person with tone is not badly disturbed by passions. Following it further beyond temperament it turns out to be, to a large extent, a particular climate of the soul. As the Czech

75

architect Honzig says in speaking of the final form of a building, "It is a condition of rest."

Whichever kind of order teachers think about, tone is still qualified by the same three things: the personality of the teacher, the personality of the children, and the method used.

I know a teacher who takes tone with her wherever she goes; whether to the infant department of a big school, to an outsized choir in the municipal or to a Red Cross demonstration in a shop window. Whether you meet her in a drawing room, in an infant room, in the street or backstage, you meet tone too. Also I know a headmaster who doesn't have to try to bring a feeling of peace upon the standards, and I've had two out of six juniors who, although they knew nothing of the conscious cultivation of tone, nevertheless carried it about in their pockets. But none of these people is discomforted with "restless passions that would not be stilled." And they have tone; inside and out.

Happily, however, the structure of a teacher is not the whole of the formula for tone in a classroom. There's the tone of the children and the tone of the district. On the east coast, where our neighbors were Sir Apirana Ngata on one side and Reweti Kohere on the other, no upheaval in the school could shake its tone. Whatever the incident, and we were not without them, the tone remained unscratched. The district itself had tone. The people had sitting among them authentic leaders and all remained well. There was serenity. If flowed down from "The Sir" through the Ngatiporou like the influence of a headmaster through his school.

But here, where there never has been a leader and where the Maoris walk precariously the tightrope between the brown and the white, there is none of the tribal confidence and cohesion of the coast. So there's no order or calm in the district, and if a teacher can't supply the missing quality from his own resources or by his own method the days can turn into outlawry.

But not necessarily, for tone can be won. Even when it is missing in the teacher and missing in the children. There's method left. The thing is to forget about appearances and cultivate the order in the unconscious. Which

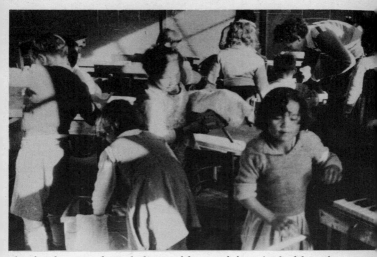

is simple enough and done with creativity. And although the room will seem disorderly by sight, it is not so by feel. Through the vents of creativity forces can get out and away, leaving the lower levels relatively calm. There's a noisy kind of peace throughout the long creative periods in the morning when every child is engrossed in some medium of construction. True, this infant room is fed by a loud-mouthed and disintegrated pa, but I don't feel hopeless. You can put every subject into the creative vent so that there will be a flow and a release of forces all day. The noise is terrible, but you've got to pay in some way. I sort out the unseemly habits and train seemly ones. I rehearse the periods in mind before we have them. I try to get reciprocal respect and trust between me and them. I go to any lengths in the pursuit of style in their work and continually check up on the feel of the room. All of which another teacher possessing natural tone doesn't need to do. But in spite of the unrest in the tribe and the lack of cohesion in the pa and the "fire that on my bosom preys," I get a precarious sense of some deep order.

And then, when you come to think about it, you find that of the two kinds of order, the conscious and the unconscious order, only one is real. It's the order in the deep hidden places. And whatever the temperament of the teacher and of the children, it is accessible to anyone. When we trace tone beyond the area of temperament and beyond the climate of the personality to its origin, we find that it is simply this order. The true order in the depths. The "still centre."

WORKBOOK

Teachers say they need their workbooks.

They say, I can't rely on myself in the melee of a lesson to work out sequences on the spot. When the time comes I need everything at my fingertips. I've got to have it all thought out beforehand.

Conception in tranquillity can range from the conscious condensation of material and method up to the level of prayer. All the great teachers of the past have drawn their action from non-action. From Christ upon the high mountain, through Lo Tung over his tea, down to us. And I can never see that these names are too big to be used side by side with today. The intention is the same —teaching. It's not this conception in tranquillity that is the point of departure.

I know that the preparation of a workbook may clarify to a teacher what he is thinking about. I know that the order and method of it reflect inescapably upon the minds of the children. And I suspect from what I see that the very fact of a workbook evokes on the mind of a teacher a reliable peace. And that its notes mean that necessary steppingstone between his conception and his execution. Indeed, I can believe comfortably enough that the assessment of a workbook can be truthfully close to the assessment of a man. It is neither the fact of a workbook nor its phase in teaching that is the point of departure. It's the incorrigible variety in man himself.

For some teachers just don't see a workbook in this way. True, they see it in the same place between conception and execution, but not as a steppingstone. To some teachers the workbook is the middleman intercepting come of the energy and glamour directed upon the canvas. Leonardo da Vinci cut straight into his marble, Rabindranath Tagore wrote his verses neat, and I didn't hear of Jesus making notes. Teachers, all of them in one medium or another, who mistrusted the middleman.

To the extent that a teacher is an artist, and according to Plato there should be no distinction, his inner eye has the native power, unatrophied, to hold the work he means to do. And in the places where he can't see, he has a trust in himself that he will see it, either in time for the occasion or eventually. And he would rather risk a blank in his teaching than expend cash on the middleman. He wants the feel of the glamour of direct engagement. He wants to see in his mind, as he teaches, the idea itself, rather than the page it is written on. He wants to work from conception itself directly upon the children without interference from the image of its record on a book. He wants to work in a way that to him is clear, without conflict and without interception.

It doesn't always, I think, clarify a teacher's thoughts to note them down. To some it is a pinioning. Something to evade. I learned when I was a very small girl that you could leave half your meaning behind in a preparatory sketch. When I was very young I worked straight from my mind upon the clay. Then I knew that what I did was all of what I could do and not just the residue of a trial. And when in teaching I found that I was required to precede all my work with the written notes of a workbook, it was with gross payment to the middleman that I did so.

In an infant room, however. where the activity is wholly expressive, with all subjects allowed their legitimate entry into the area of creativity, the question of a workbook can hardly arise. Wherever there's creativity on a large scale there's life, and I, anyway, can't plot life. I just join in. How are we to know what is going to come from the children on this day or that? How can I tell what the reading and spelling is going to be since each morning they write their own books for the day's use? Does a teacher wish to anticipate the purposes of each new day? In an infant room cultivating the organic expansion, a teacher learns to put the factors of mood and change before the prognostications of a workbook.

As Caldwell Cook says: "Not the professor, but the artist, is your true school master."

DANCING

Dancing I place in the morning output time, considering it as good a medium as any other, since Plato said it was the one complete expression involving the faculties on all levels, spiritual, intellectual and physical. That's what I think too. Not that I deliberately teach it for that reason. It just happened one bright spring morning when I was playing some Schubert to please no one but myself that a child stood up from his work and began composing a dance, then another, then another, and there it all was. And here it all still is.

Although most of the interpretations come from them, I indulge myself by providing them with a further selection of movements to use as they choose, to supplement their own movements. But I haven't noticed much of it being used voluntarily in their interpretation of new music. The old story of imposition again.

I never use other than classical music. Not only for my own sake but because it was a classic that brought them to their feet in the first place. So far I have used Schubert, Beethoven, Tchaikovsky, Chopin, Brahms and Grieg. But I'm only feeling my way, since my only source of dancing knowledge is from my own dreaming.

My aim is that a child may be able to create dancing as freely as he draws or writes autobiography or plays. But I haven't got there yet.* Although we place dancing in the output period, we also use it to break any strain of work during the day.

---

* By the time I wrote *Spinster* I had got there.

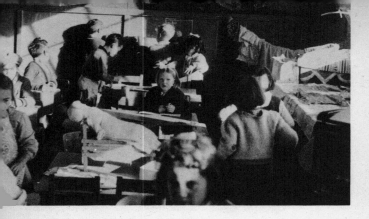

The Unlived Life

It's all so merciful on a teacher, this appearance of the subjects of an infant room in the creative vent. For one thing, the drive is no longer the teacher's but the children's own. And for another, the teacher is at last with the stream and not against it: the stream of children's inexorable creativeness. As Dr. Jung says, psychic life is a world power that exceeds by many times all the powers of the earth; as Dr. Burrow says, the secret of our collective ills is to be traced to the suppression of creative ability; and as Erich Fromm says, destructiveness is the outcome of the unlived life.

So it is of more than professional moment that all of the work of young children should be through the creative vent. It is more than a teaching matter or a dominion one. It's an international matter. So often I have said in the past, when a war is over the statesmen should not go into conference with one another but should turn their attention to the infant rooms, since it is from there that comes peace or war. And that's how I see organic teaching. It helps to set the creative pattern in a mind while it is yet malleable, and in this role is a humble contribution to peace.

The expansion of a child's mind can be a beautiful growth. And in beauty are included the qualities of equilibrium, harmony and rest. There's no more comely word in the language than "rest." All the movement in life, and out of it too, is towards a condition of rest. Even the simple movement of a child "coming up."

I can't disassociate the activity in an infant room from peace and war. So often I have seen the destructive vent, beneath an onslaught of creativity, dry up under my eyes. Especially with the warlike Maori five-year-olds who pass through my hands in hundreds, arriving with no other thought in their heads other than to take, break, fight and be first. With no opportunity for creativity they may well develop, as they did in the past, with fighting as their ideal of life. Yet all this can be expelled through the creative vent, and the more violent the boy the more I see that he creates, and when he kicks the others with his big boots, treads on fingers on the mat, hits another over the head with a piece of wood or throws a stone, I put clay in his hands, or chalk. He can create bombs if he likes or draw my house in flame, but it is the creative vent that is widening all the time and the destructive one atrophying, however much it may look to the contrary. And anyway I have always been more afraid of the weapon unspoken than of the one on a blackboard.

With all this in mind therefore I try to bring as many facets of teaching into the creative vent as possible, with emphasis on reading and writing. And that's just what organic teaching is; all subjects in the creative vent. It's just as easy for a teacher, who gives a child a brush and lets him paint, to give him a pencil and let him write, and to let him pass his story to the next one to read. Sim-

plicity is so safe. There's no occasion whatever for the early imposition of a dead reading, a dead vocabulary. I'm so afraid of it. It's like a frame over a young tree making it grow in an unnatural shape. It makes me think of that curtailment of a child's expansion of which Erich Fromm speaks, of that unlived life of which destructiveness is the outcome. "And instead of the wholeness of the expansive tree we have only the twisted and stunted bush." The trouble is that a child from a modern respectable home suffers such a serious frame on his behaviour long before he comes near a teacher. Nevertheless I think that after a year of organic work the static vocabularies can be used without misfortune. They can even, under the heads of external stimulus and respect for the standard of English, become desirable.

But only when built upon the organic foundation. And there's hardly anything new in the conception of progress from the known to the unknown. It's just that when the inorganic reading is imposed first it interferes with integration; and it's upon the integrated personality that everything is built. We've lost the gracious movement from the inside outward. We overlook the footing. I talk sometimes about a bridge from the pa to the European environment, but there is a common bridge for a child of any race and of more moment than any other: the bridge from the inner world outward. And that is what organic teaching is. An indispensable step in integration. Without it we get this one-patterned mind of the New Zealand child, accruing from so much American influence of the mass-mind type. I think that we already have so much pressure towards sameness through radio, film and comic outside the school, that we can't afford to do a thing inside that is not toward individual development, and from this stance I can't see that we can indulge in the one imposed reading for all until the particular variety of a mind is set. And a cross-section of children from different places in New Zealand provides me with an automatic check on the progress of the one-patterned mind. (I own seventy fancy-dress costumes which I lend.) All the children want the same costumes. If you made dozens of cowboy and cowgirl costumes, hundreds of Superman and thousands of Rocket Man costumes and hired them

84

at half a guinea a go, you'd get every penny of it and would make a fortune vast enough to retire on and spend the rest of your life in the garden. As for my classics— Bo-Peep, the Chinese Mandarin, Peter Pan and the Witch and so on—they so gather the dust that they have had to be folded and put away. It's this sameness in children that can be so boring. So is death boring.

To write peaceful reading books and put them in an infant room is not the way to peace. They don't even scratch the surface. No child ever asked for a Janet or a John costume. There is only one answer to destructiveness and that is creativity. And it never was and never will be any different. And when I say so I am in august company.

The noticeable thing in New Zealand society is the body of people with their inner resources atrophied. Seldom have they had to reach inward to grasp the thing that they wanted. Everything, from material requirements to ideas, is available ready-made. From mechanical gadgets in the shops to sensation in the films they can buy almost anything they fancy. They can buy life itself from the film and radio—canned life.

And even if they tried to reach inward for something that maybe they couldn't find manufactured, they would no longer find anything there. They've dried up. From babyhood they have had shiny toys put in their hands,

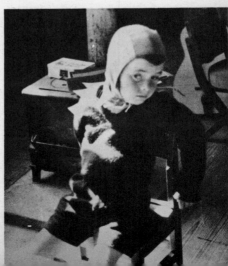

and in the kindergartens and infant rooms bright pictures and gay material. Why conceive anything of their own? There has not been the need. The capacity to do so has been atrophied and now there is nothing there. The vast expanses of the mind that could have been alive with creative activity are now no more than empty vaults that must, for comfort's sake, be filled with non-stop radio, and their conversation consists of a list of platitudes and clichés.

I can't quite understand why.

From what I see of modern education the intention is just the opposite: to let children grow up in their own personal way into creative and interesting people. Is it the standard textbooks? Is it the consolidation? Is it the quality of the teachers? Is it the access to film and radio and the quality of those luxuries? Or is it the access to low-grade reading material infused through all of these things? I don't know where the intention fails but we end up with the same pattern of a person in nine hundred ninety-nine instances out of a thousand.

I said to a friend of mine, a professor, recently, "What kind of children arrive at the University to you?" He said, "They're all exactly the same." "But," I said, "how can it be like that? The whole plan of primary education at least is for diversity." "Well," he answered, "they come to me like samples from a mill. Not one can think for himself. I beg them not to serve back to me exactly what I have given to them. I challenge them sometimes with wrong statements to provoke at least some disagreement but even that won't work." "But," I said, "you must confess to about three per cent originality." "One in a thousand," he replied. "One in a thousand."

On the five-year-old level the mind is not yet patterned and it is an exciting thought. True, I often get the over-disciplined European five, crushed beyond recognition as an identity, by respectable parents, but never Maoris; as a rule a five-year-old child is not boring. In an infant room it is still possible to meet an interesting, unpatterned person. "In the infant room," I told this professor, "we still have identity. It's somewhere between my infant-room level and your university level that the story breaks. But I don't think it is the plan of education itself."

I think that the educational story from the infant room to the university is like the writing of a novel. You can't be sure of your beginning until you have checked it with your ending. What might come of infant teachers visiting the university and professors visiting the infant room? I had two other professors in my infant room last year and they proved themselves to be not only delightfully in tune but sensitively helpful.

Yet what I believe and what I practise are not wholly the same thing. For instance, although I have reason to think that a child's occupation until seven should not be other than creative in the many mediums, nevertheless I find myself teaching some things.

With all this in mind, therefore, the intent of the infant room is the nurturing of the organic idea,

the preservation of the inner resources,

the exercise of the inner eye and

the protraction of the true personality.

I like unpredictability and variation; I like drama and I like gaiety; I like peace in the world and I like interesting people, and all this means that I like life in its organic shape and that's just what you get in an infant room where the creative vent widens. For this is where style is born in both writing and art, for art is the way you do a thing and an education based on art at once flashes out style.

The word "jalopy" made its fascinating appearance the other day. Brian wrote, "I went to town. I came back on a jalopy bus." This word stirred us. The others cross-questioned him on the character of such a bus. It turned out to mean "rackety" and although the word was picked up at once nevertheless they still ask for it to go up on the spelling list. We haven't had "jalopy" for spelling lately, Brian says. He loves spelling it, which is what I mean when I say that the drive is the children's own. It's all so merciful on a teacher.

Inescapably war and peace wait in an infant room; wait and vie.

True the toy shops are full of guns, boys' hands hold tanks and war planes while the blackboards, clay boards and easels burst with war play. But I'm unalarmed. My

concern is the rearing of the creative disposition, for creativity in this crèche of living where people can still be changed must in the end defy, if not defeat, the capacity for destruction. Every happening in the infant room is either creative or destructive; every drawing, every shaping, every sentence and every dance goes one way or the other. For, as Erich Fromm says, "life has an inner dynamism of its own; it tends to grow, to be expressed, to be lived. The amount of destructiveness in a child is proportionate to the amount to which the expansiveness of his life has been curtailed. Destructiveness is the outcome of the unlived life."

I believe in this as passionately as the artist in his brush and the roadman in his shovel. For every work, and first of all that of a teacher, must have its form, its design. And the design of my work is that creativity in this time of life when character can be influenced forever is the solution to the problem of war. To me it has the validity of a law of physics and all the unstatable, irrepressible emotion of beauty.

Daily Rhythm

9—10:45 BREATHE OUT

Conversation   Crying
 Painting   Quarrelling
  Creative Writing Blocks
ORGANIC Clay   Creative Dancing
   Sand   Key Vocabulary
WORK Water   Organic Vocabulary
    Paste paint Dolls
FOR   Doll's washing Boats
     Singing Chalk
MORNING   Day-dreaming Loving

11–12 BREATHE IN

 Key Vocabulary ¼ hr. for Little Ones
 Organic Vocabulary
 Organic reading
  Organic discussion
  Stories, pictures, picture books for
         Little Ones

1–2 BREATHE OUT

 Golden Section   STANDARD
 Plastic media for Little Ones

2:10–3 BREATHE IN   WORK

 Standard vocabulary
 Standard reading
  Maori book vocabulary FOR
  Maori book read
   Supplementary reading
   Stories, songs, poems AFTERNOON
   Letters for Little Ones

Life in a Maori School

—from a dairy

And how are you getting on with the Maoris? I ask a visiting teacher to the school.

Oh, it's the energy that's the trouble. They're always on the go. But once you've got your foot on their neck they're all right.

I understand . . . I understand. . . .

I do. But I don't talk about it. I don't try to describe to others the force of the energy in our New Race. Indeed, when I speak of it as "force of energy" I'm grossly under-stating it. It's more like a volcano in continuous eruption. To stand on it, in my Maori infant room anyway, to stand on it with both feet and teach it in quiet orthodoxy would be a matter of murders and madnesses and spirit-ual deaths, while to teach it without standing on it is an utter impossibility. The only way I know of dealing with it is to let it teach itself. And that's what I've been forced to do.

And that's exactly what I do. I stand back, something like a chairman, and let it teach itself. The only thing I step forward to teach is style. And believe me, I teach that. I teach it all the time in everything, because the rest follows. I teach style, and only style.

You're got to be either brave or desperate to take this road, even though in the end it leads to wide and happy fields. And I'm not brave. But I've got to the wide and happy fields. I'm all too aware that they are noisy fields, since my teacher's mind has been set by the past into the tradition of silence. But they're the only fields that I can understand and believe in, I being so simple—and even though the price is professional isolation and ineradi-cable, inescapable and corrosive guilt, here we stay.

For long sitting, watching and pondering (all so un-professional) I have found out the worst enemies to what we call teaching. There are two.

The first is the children's interest in each other. It plays the very devil with orthodox methods. If only they'd stop talking to each other, playing with each other, fight-ing with each other and loving each other. This unseemly and unlawful communication! In self-defence I've got to use the damn thing. So I harness the communication, since I can't control it, and base my method on it. They read in pairs, sentence and sentence about. There's no time for either to get bored. Each checks the other's mis-takes and hurries him up if he's too slow, since after all his own turn depends on it. They teach each other all their work in pairs, sitting cross-legged knee to knee on the mat, or on their tables, arguing with, correcting, abusing or smiling at each other. And between them all the time is this togetherness, so that learning is so mixed up with relationship that it becomes part of it. What an unsung creative medium is relationship!

The other trouble with this New Race is their desire to make things. If only they'd sit like the white children with their hands still and wait until they're told to do something and told how to do it. The way they draw bombers and make them with anything and roar around the room with them.

Noise, noise, noise, yes. But if you don't like noise, don't be a teacher. Because children are noisy animals and these in particular, the young of a New Race, the noisiest I have ever known. But it's a natural noise and therefore bearable. True, there is an occasional howl of rage, a shout of accusation, soprano crying and the sound of something falling, but there is also a voice raised in joy, someone singing and the break, break, break of laughter. In any case it's all expulsion of energy and as such, a help. I let anything come . . . within safety; but *I use it.*

I use everything. They write their own books every morning for a start, to read when reading time comes. And the reading time . . . ah well, this is getting into the matter of method again and I'll get myself led miles away from what I'm talking about: the foot on the neck.

The spirit is so wild with the lid off. I'm still learning how to let it fly and yet to discipline it. It's got to be disciplined in a way that's hard to say. It still must have its range and its wing . . . it must still be free to dare the gale and sing, but it's got to come home at the right time and nest in the right place. For the spirit to live its freest, the mind must acknowledge discipline. In this room anyway. In this room there is an outer discipline as well as an inner. They've got to listen to me when I speak and obey what I speak. I can only say that I don't often speak. And that I carefully weigh what I do speak. But the track between these two conditions, the spiritual freedom and the outer discipline, is narrower than any tightrope, and seldom can I say that I have walked it.

The volcanic energy, precipitated from the combustion of the old race and the young, the volcanic energy of the

New Race blows—but is directed. It was exhausting at first, this controlling of the direction of the blasts; and not without risks, this changing of the vents, for the young Maori warriors are full of "take, break, fight, and be first" when they come; but it is not as exhausting or as dangerous as standing in the way of it. Sometimes when a tribal excitement surges through the school, the tidal emotion rises up to the level of our eyes and over our sign-posts so that we think as we drown, "the foot on the neck." But I know that there is too much material and too much drive in the wake of these floods, so we hold our breath and rely on the inner disciplines. At least it's life. For both them and me. And the creative work that comes from it, especially the books, is something I'd pay any-thing for.

Yet I'm a disciplinarian. It's just that I like the lid off. I like seeing what's there. I like unpredictability and gaiety and interesting people, however small, and funny things happening and wild things happening and sweet, and everything that life is, uncovered. I hate covers of any kind. I like the true form of living, even in school. I'm in love with the organic shape.

"They're all right once you've got your foot on their neck."

I understand. I understand. But communication and creativity are abler teachers than a foot.

But I'm still no nearer to describing this energy. It has to be seen to be understood; the energy when the lid's off, I mean. And I don't talk about it either; so insignificant a thing as an infant room of the young of a minority race, in a small country, on a paltry planet, in a comparatively junior universe. It's too mere. It's enough for myself that "The least thing stirs me; the greatest cannot make me quake."

My newest little white boy, Mark, came up to me this morning. "My apron's pinched," he said with a mixture of excitement and resignation.

"Don't say that!" I replied warmly, forgetting my laboriously learnt infant-room patience. "We don't take things here!"

He looked so smug. The characteristic offspring of the

smug middle-class ignorance. "Well it's not in my desk. I put it in there."

"I told you," I replied, still dangerously warm, across a moving pattern of brown faces and above a sustained chord of young voices, "to take it home on Friday to get it washed. It'll be at home."

"It's not at home."

"It'll be in your bag then."

"It's not." But conversations in the vitality of a Maori infant room don't, can't, last long. Both voices and movement bore him away from our outer eye as well as my inner.

"Primed at home!" I said passionately over the lunch table, where infant-room patience was shed. "He didn't even look for it! They never do, the white ones! There's only one explanation of a missing article in a Maori community where a *Pakeha** is concerned. Stolen! This child hasn't been with me a week so how can he have found out for himself whether or not the Maori children steal?"

"Really," said K., cutting up his tomato, "it does make you wonder how far we can get when the homes are so set."

"Mrs. Henderson, someone's pinched my duster!"

Another white one. I looked up from Matawhero's reading, feeling my neck reddening. . . .

"It—it—it's in his desk!" spluttered Matawhero with anxiety.

"He didn't even look for it," I told K. as the senior girls washed the infant-room floor, "and he's been with me a month or two and could have found out for himself by now whether or not the Maori children steal."

K. replied reflectively, "The school seems to have made no headway in that home."

"He hadn't even looked for it."

"Yes. It makes you wonder."

I was busy after school on my third edition of infant readers for Maoris when K. put his head through the door of my workroom at the back of the house and said,

* *Pakeha:* white person.

94

"I've brought two Maori ladies in for afternoon tea. Mrs. Rameke and another."

I put down my brush, since Mrs. Rameke was a sensitive and intelligent Maori. Many of them were for that matter. But this one was the Welfare Officer, and moreover had in her just enough extra of something, maybe white blood, maybe Maori ranking blood, to help her to succeed in the European way of life. Or to what, I remarked privately, to what was success in the Pakeha eye. It depended on what you called "success."

They were fingering instinctively the ancient Kiwi raincloak that I was minding for a homeless Maori friend of mine and were exclaiming at the Maori rafter patterns on my curtains when I came into the drawing room. It made me so happy. "Ah!" I called as I came in. "Trust a Maori to appreciate that!"

In no time the conversation was leaping like canoes with the tide. Like the Great Canoes that mastered the vast oceans six hundred years ago to deliver the Polynesian seed to the Land of the Long White Cloud. . . .

"It's not that I'm anti-Pakeha," I protested. "I love my own race. It's just that knowing the Maoris so well I see the many unfairnesses. And they do—" I felt within for the right word—"sting."

"Ah," they breathed with that inimitable Maori sympathy, in that way Maoris have of following along everything you say, feeling everything you say, and being so obvious about it. It carried me further. "It's my white children who so clearly reveal the attitude in the European homes about. The Maori children are most conclusively prejudged. Actually, there's a most wonderful cross in this pa. These children are easily the most vital and the most intelligent of any children, brown or white, that

95

we have ever handled. And it's not only we who say so. The Phys Ed man, and the Art man and the inspectors all say the same thing."

"Yes," said Mrs. Rameke. "There's a very deep breach between the Maori and Pakeha in this district."

"It makes us," said the other, "very shy and sensitive. If only the Europeans knew how appreciative we are of the slightest help. But the attitude against us makes us afraid to speak."

"In my work, though," said Mrs. Rameke, speaking thoughtfully in perfect English but declaring her Maori origin unmistakably in the fluent accompaniment of her hands, "I have found that it is only the one class that shows racial prejudice. It's this . . . this . . . what do you call it? . . . this middle class The lower tens" (Ah, she had fallen, as so many Maoris fall, on the issue of plurals) "have sympathy and I find that the academic people, the aa . . upper people . . . always understand. They want to. They try to. . . ."

A bad day for the New Race. This long-drawn-out disgrace of being a Maori is continually confused in my mind with images of the great Rangatiras of the past and their proud people. I see the high and decorated prows of great canoes rising to wave crests; the poignant beauty of pas, relaxed in the setting of trees and running water; hear the cries of battle frenzy and the speeches, cadenced like river talk. But what do my white parents know of that? How can I protect my beautiful Matawhero from the *taiaha** of prejudice?

"Education," spoke Sir Maui Pomare, before he departed to greet his ancestors, "is the new paddle of the Maori canoe."

"Kin Oi go outsoide?" asked Matawhero. I'm getting used to the horrible pronunciation the Maoris pick up here in a white district. Although when I first came down from the fastnesses of Waio, where the Maori vowels were pure, it was as painful as a creaking door. I looked down at him. He was very small. I knelt to his level. It wasn't time to go out yet.

"Kin Oi?" he whined again.

---

* *taiaha:* wooden Maori spear.

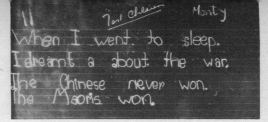

When I went to sleep.
I dreamt a about the war.
The Chinese never won.
The Maoris won.

Well, I thought, it's my fault if he wants to go outside. Something wrong with my infant room. But it's uncomfortable shedding tradition. It's so warm and without it I feel so cold. "Have you done your work?" I said.

He scattered away and brought it. Screwed-up-little-writing-all-stuck-together-at-a-rising-angle.

"Kin Oi go?"

"Yes. Why not." ·

"Everyone go to sleep."

"Aren't you going to read 'The B'ue Jug,' Mrs. Hen'son?"

"Do we have to go to sleep?"

"Matawhero, go to sleep! Mrs. Hen'son said we got to go to sleep!"

"Read 'The B'ue Jug,' Mrs. Hen'son."

"Mrs. Hen'son, Rangi won't go to sleep!"

"Do we got to lie down? Twinnie, lie down!"

"Aren't you going to read 'The B'ue Jug'?"

"Twinnie's eyes are open! She's looking through her eyes!"

"The other Twinnie's eyes are open!"

"Not!"

" 'Course!"

"Not!"

" 'Course!"

"What about 'The B'ue Jug,' Mrs. Hen'son?"

"Go to sleep!"

Silence.

Mark: Mrs. Hen'son, I can't draw any of those things in that story.

Me: You could draw the rope, I suppose.

Mark: Just a straight line?

Me: Yes. Then the rat. Just a round thing like that and a line for a tail like that.

97

Mark: Just a little round thing for a head and a little round thing for the stomach and a line for the tail?

Me: And a few legs. Tame, blow your nose. Junior, tuck your shirt in.

Twin: Mrs. Hen'son. Twinnie is cheeky. She's drawing on my side.

Mark: And a few legs?

Me: And a dot for his eye.

Rangi came and stared raptly at this where I pinned it on the wall beside me. Then I heard that unbearable throat noise that boys make to indicate gunfire. It cut through the spontaneous singing in the room. That wretched new boy drawing his guns. I went over and smacked the calf of his leg as hard as I could, forgetting my fingers for the Schubert Andante. "Don't make that noise!"

Then Mark made another rat.

"Give that to Rangi." It might give white Mark a kind feeling to Maori Rangi.

Then another rat.

"Give that one to . . . aa . . . Matawhero."

Wiki brought up a page of drawing. "Who did that?" I said.

"My mate."

"Who's your mate?"

"Naomi."

"She's a kind girl."

"Can I have a scissors to cut it out?"

"No. You make your own rat. Then you can have some scissors."

"I can't make a rat."

"Mark can." I showed her Mark's on the wall.

Mark made another rat. "I'll give it to Tame, Mrs. Hen'son."

Matawhero didn't do any drawing. He was reading "The Blue Jug" to Patchy on the step. Brown reading to white. More toleration, a little more interracial understanding maybe. Composing it from the pictures, Matawhero is too desperately concerned with the personal relation to do anything with only himself in it. (Which is why I like his grandfather.) So is Patchy.

Wiki: I've done my piggy, Mrs. Hen'son.

Me: Where's its legs?

She turned it round another way. "Here's some legs. Can I have a scissors?"

"Yes. You can have some scissors."

Mark made another rat.

Patchy: Mrs. Hen'son, is it hometime?

Matawhero: Mrs. H. It was me rang the bell! I rang it three times!

Others: Mrs. Hen'son, here's the pussy!

Mrs. H., can I take primer one?

Mrs. H., can I play the piano?

Mrs. H., Patchy took my paper I had ready for after play!

Then Hirani began playing "Pokare Kare Ana" and the singing drowned most of it. . . .

The abstract pattern of behaviour. The organic design, almost. Behaviour in the raw. Clues. Clues to the hidden sources of adult action. Confessing them.

Matawhero: Kin Oi sit with Gordon again?

Gordon, white and pleased: You're always wanting to sit with me!

Me, privately: Score.

But I don't expect the brown and the white to ever really mix. All I'm playing for is understanding. It's not that they can't mix on any of the spiritual, intellectual or physical levels. I have done that myself. It's in the sphere of interest that they divide. The interests of each race grown from the separate centuries behind. The Maoris, *generally speaking*, love tribal gatherings with emphasis on food and spiritual matters. While we, featuring the intellect, are segregating irretrievably. Only generally speaking, this. Particularly, my highest encounters have been with a being who was brown.

White Harry is home because brown Junior gave him a hiding. Reverse. But I don't belive that it is the hiding alone that has sent him home. Just a rhythmic reaction to his passionate absorption in school for these first few months. There has to be a swing back sometime. Actually I told his mother at the beginning that when she saw the signs to keep him home for a rest. "Although Mr. Henderson won't agree with me on that," I added. But I could have saved the retreat if I had been all there and not still in a no-man's-land after a sharp weekend. I could have done the comforting myself as I have done before. But I fell down on that and there is Harry home and I'm ashamed. True I could have had the bully strapped, there's only one treatment for big, ignorant bullies and that's to feel their own skin sting, but I didn't, and Harry is home and as an infant mistress I failed and am regretful. Even though as a person I was sufficiently in character. Slowly descending from a moment . . . there is a . . . an allowable blindness.

Brown Waiwini can't even see a story through without getting up and coming to me for her communication. This art of communication. When we have stifled the symbol of it and suppressed the desire for it we have achieved respectability. Joy said, "How I hate respectability!" A lot of Waiwini's work does not get done because of this preoccupation with the personal relation but I honour it and cultivate it knowing that this is the stuff that the "meaning" is made of. Such a warm, observant creature. She gets as close as is humanly possible to whatever's happening and to whomever it is happening to. Like Matawhero. At the tangi for Whareparita's twin babies she edged herself to the top of the two tiny coffins and hung over the two tiny dead faces in complete self-forgetfulness. And self-forgetfulness is one of the exquisitenesses of living. And Waiwini and Matawhero are *livers* in full measure. Not too much of what we call work, of course, but ah, the living they accomplish!

This afternoon marks the beginning of composition. Word composition. Writing. The first wall between one liver and another. Putting thoughts in writing for the other instead of the direct route of speech or touch. I'm both gratified and sad. Talkers and touchers are never lonely but writers are. Here is the beginning of loneliness. Should I be glad because my children are voluntarily composing sentences for the first time? One Twinnie is writing on the blackboard about the story: "The fish is jumped. The fish is swimming. The little fish is in the sea. The fish he have no leg." Ah well I can't stop civilisation. A picture springs into the world behind my eyes of a Maori *marae**
of the past with the tattooed, impassioned speakers. The direct vital communication at all times.

I have taken to singing to them when they are lying with their eyes closed resting. Songs my father sang to us at bedtime. Songs that under the stress of teaching I didn't have time to sing to my own children . . . at least not very often. They like it and I like it. I sing all his songs. And get rid of a good deal of something, I don't know what.

* *marae:* a temple enclosure used for sacred ceremonies.

Oh where oh where has my little dog gone,
Oh where oh where can he be?
With his hair cut short and his tail cut long,
Oh where oh where can he be?

Oh going down the river in the old steam boat . . .

I won't finish that one as it belongs exclusively to our family and has for centuries. But somehow I can't help singing it to these sleepy brown children.

I burnt most of my infant-room material on Friday. I say that the more material there is for a child, the less pull there is on his own resources. Other children coming to me from other schools are most annoyingly helpless. They want the teacher to do everything for them like a mother. I don't believe in shiny polished blocks. The shine and the colour should be supplied by the child's own imagination. Maybe he will not imagine polish and shine. In which case the polish and colour supplied externally is obviously an *imposition*. Which I scream is deadly! Whatever his own imagination *does* supply will be something in character with his own needs. Which is integral, cohesive and organic. I speak of blocks as an example but only symbolically. I mean all the other contraptions. Mrs. S. for example was given the job of preparing mountains of reading cards to supplement the new reading books. Pictures for every word. Pictures illustrating, *believe it or not,* words like "up," "to," "my" . . . over and above the nouns. It's terribly hard to believe that modern teachers can do this and modern inspectors instigate it. Can't a child picture his own nouns when he hears them? Do we have pictures of prepositions and conjunctions? And beyond all this think of the *time* it takes to care for all this stuff. Only infant teachers know the time it takes to keep this stuff in order and in repair. Time that could be used in precious conversation with them. I burnt all the work of my youth. Dozens of cards made of three-ply, and hand-printed and illustrated. Boxes of them. There will be only the following list in my infant room:

102

Chalk	Books
Blackboards	Charts
Paper	Paints
Pencils	Clay
Guitar	Piano

And when a child wants to read he can pick up a book with his own hands and struggle through it. The removal of effort and the denying to the child of its right to *call on its own resources*. . . .

(I was sad though, seeing it all go up in smoke.)

But teaching is so much simpler and clearer as a result. There's much more time for conversation. Conversation . . . communication. (You should have heard the roaring in the chimney!)

We had our grading this week. The men were well marked, Tom and K., but as usual I was very low. There's no doubt about it. I am a very low-ability teacher. My sister Daphne says on this matter that it would be a disgrace for a woman in my position to be a good teacher. As for myself, maybe it is a distinction of some kind to be unacceptable in New Zealand teaching. I walk alone, like Edmund Burke. We are "rogues," the term critics give to people they can't classify. That's the alternative assumption. I use both.

Saturday morning. I have come to a decision this morning. I'm resigning at the end of this year. I have established, begun so much here. Everything of myself I have put in here. But I'm going to leave it. I've had enough. I'm going to be a wife and nothing more. I may even leave earlier. I'm going to find out how much sick leave I have left and will use that first.

The grass is growing a little now on Whareparita's twin babies in the little cemetery at the corner. And I think the grass is growing a little on Whareparita's sorrow. It made me sad for a while after she had come home from the hospital to see her across the road taking up her old duties about the house again. Sometimes I would see her leaning in the front door with a very idle broom, just looking. And someone said to me, "Whareparita was down at the cemetery yesterday crying over her little grave." So I thought, surely I can do something for her. It seemed too hard for a girl of sixteen to meet such a blow. So I thought, I'll take her with me whenever I can. I'll take her into town with me on Friday night. But I forgot of course, and as I was walking down the street on Friday night through the crowds, I met Whareparita, all painted up and ready for more action. With another girl. Really, I thought, you'd never know by the look of her that there were two darling little babies at the bottom of a deep grave at home and a married man lurking somewhere in the background, reflecting, maybe, and wondering. But the illness and sadness did something to Whareparita for all that. She was a rough-skinned, ordinary Maori girl before but now her skin texture is wonderful and her figure even more so. She came second in the Beauty Contest last month. Then the other day a truck pulled up across the way and Whareparita got out. She had overalls rolled up beneath her knees and bare feet. What a pretty sight!

"I like you," says Mohi, "because you smoke."
Mohi is a very fair Maori whose father is a wandering Dodgems man from the Carnival.
"Of course I smoke."
"You'll go to Satan."
"I hope so."
"I smoke," he says.
"What . . . you're going to Satan too?"
He nods seriously, Maori fashion.
"All right, me and you, Mohi. Let's both pack up off to Satan."
Not past him though.

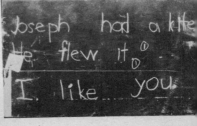

The only major thing that happened last week at school was the cleanness of little Hine and Riti Tamati. Someone had bathed these children and washed their hair and combed it and tied it. Their clothes were clean and ironed. I was astonished. I myself have been taking their clothes off and washing them and combing their hair in self-defence.

"Who washed you?" I said.

"Mummy," they said.

"Is she back?"

"Yea. She camed back. She wash our clothes."

"Was it she who did your hair?"

"Yea. She does our hair. She camed back."

"Well well! Look at that!"

I haven't said anything about these two yet because I wanted to write about Rose first, their big sister who allegedly cares for them when their mother is away. But I haven't got round to Rose yet. That was Rose in the white shorts who led the Beauty Parade on Gala Day.

I'm not resigning. I've changed my mind. What I call my mind.

Harry reappeared this morning. Masses of tears. They concentrated on keeping him at school until I arrived. This is never before the second bell. So I just picked him up and sat him on the table beside me and he watched me talking to the others over their work and played with the stamps. Also I read "The Blue Jug." He told me that he was to stay home in the afternoon to have a sleep as the new baby had kept him awake all night. But he came after all in the afternoon. And seemed to be very happy. But I think he is feeling the tension of the home. Four little ones. Especially so young and being the first of four.

Think of the repeated ousting from his first place with his mother. So . . . I mothered him, or grandmothered him if you like. Besidés I had a ghost to lay.

I've got all the standard girls sorted out into basketball teams. A, B and C. They are all making pockets for their blazers, the new banner, and are all knitting themselves bright yellow sports pullovers. Most of them are practising the piano. I feel satisfied that they are all mopped up and very busy. The goal throwers have a certain number of goals to achieve every day, twenty to be exact. I was dubious about this, thinking I was being hard and that it was too much, but some of the B team were getting hundreds a day and today Jane's score was five hundred and twenty. I asked the men if I was expected to believe these astronomical figures. Amiria scored seven hundred and twenty-one last week. I said to Tom, "I can't check up on them. I can do no more than accept these totals. At least they are fascinating."

My infant room nearly always has in it a boy practising, a girl sewing on the machine, a girl sewing her pocket, someone knitting and three or four dozen infants working and talking and laughing and often singing. I love to hear the singing breaking out, one first, then three, then all. But it seems that the things I like most are things that bring me disfavour. I often go to the piano myself and play their songs. Sometimes they run up and sing and sometimes just sing where they are. But when they hear

106

"Goodnight Irene," they run up and cluster round and sing with everything they've got. So much so that I am in the position to play a part. And Waiwini squeezes as near as possible to me, to the keyboard and the center of things in general and tries to follow the part. Then after a while they drift back to what they are doing. Lovely movement. Admirable grouping. Perfect, spontaneous design. Now where was I? Yes, all very bad teaching, I'm convinced.

Well now, B.'s are not handling our winter tunics. I don't blame them. I strolled into B.'s in Napier yesterday; K. was over there looking at moving picture machines for the school, and lo! What should I see but rows of brown tunics *and* blazers! So I talked about these things with a tall, efficient sales-manager woman who frightened me, who said she would order more next time. So I thought of Mrs. Hakiwai who has already paid in advance for her tunics in B.'s. So I put three aside for her. "Mrs. Hakiwai," I said. She got out her paper and pencil.

"How do you spell that?"

I spelt it.

"That's Maori!" she accused, putting down her pencil.

"Yes."

"The Maoris are very erratic. They promise to take a thing and don't come back."

"That's true. But this one won't."

"Are you the teacher?"

"Yes," I said, looking down in disgrace.

She looked me up and down. She all but said "Turn around." I thought way inside me, What a cost this dream of mine is. To have my Maoris in brown and yellow. So after all that, I had to move down to the other end of the showroom and try on some fur coats to cheer myself up.

K. was talking to the Senior Inspector the other night at a Headmaster's meeting. He told K. that he was sending me a junior next term, "to help Mrs. Henderson with all she is attempting to do." You can imagine how the other schools will rise against this interpretation of staffing rules. However there is always a storm awaiting the imaginative. The architect was out also yesterday measuring up for a staff room and a laundry and a shower room. More storm. However there it is. I have a very tiny little dream that we may make this school fit enough for the white children to come back. I have been thinking it rather a shame on someone's part that the white children should be driven from their own school and forced to all sorts of transport embarrassments in attending elsewhere.

Since B.'s have refused to handle the Fernhill School winter tunics I was . . . frustrated. I love action, not delays and refusals. I was immobilised and couldn't think what to do. And didn't do anything, being on this particular subject slightly numb. Then what should happen but wonderful new brown winter tunics began appearing in the school. Where in heaven were they coming from?

"Where did you get that?"

"My Auntie's niece made it."

"Where did you get your gym from, Marion?"

"My grandfather just finished it last night."

"Della, is that a brown gym I see on you?"

"Mrs. Hen'son, my mother bought it from Napier."

The next morning a knock at my door, and there was Lily with an immense parcel. "These are our gyms and blazers, Mrs. Henderson. My nannie bought them from Napier. Mine and Amiria's and Reremoana's. She said are they the right length?" And so on.

" 'Believe it or not' time," I told the men at morning tea in the porch, not having a staff room.

"Mrs. Henderson, Irini won't be here this afternoon."

"Why, Lotus?"

"She's in the hospital."

"What's the matter with my Irini!"

"Lawrence, he was giving her a ride home on his bike and Victoria got in the way and they dodged and fell off and Lawrence he fell on top of Irini and Irini has got two holes in her face."

"When was this?"

"At dinnertime. Then Irini's mother got a taxi and took her to the hospital."

"We'll have to go down to that hospital on Sunday," I said to K. today. "There's a lot of them there now."

"Da was operated on on Friday."

"Good gracious!"

"Dusky is resting and dieting in there after a severe heart attack a fortnight ago."

"Good gracious! I didn't know!"

"Really we must go down on Sunday."

"There's always a group of them there when I go. It's always a problem what to take them. Last time I took them all stamped envelopes."

At the Hemingway film last night I saw Whareparita (of the twins) in the dress circle with a young Maori boy. Just a matter of how long now.

K. is having demonstrations in the pa of film projectors. This adds up to several film evenings. Everybody goes. It'll be lovely having a projector.

Yesterday afternoon at 2:30 when I had my infant room busy on reading and word work, the C basketball team waiting for me out on the field, the knitting and pocket girls under way in the infant room, Hori practising on the piano, Lotus sewing her uniform and Mere pressing the pleats of the new tunics with the new iron over in the main building, I thought of the junior that the Senior Inspector was sending next term. I smiled.

The home of Puki of the cooties is across the road. It is one room. There are eight in the family, ten with the parents, and all the eight children sleep in the one bed. They come to school with their hair uncombed and their faces often dirty. The mother seems to have lost heart, as the father spends every Saturday afternoon in the pub drinking away the wages and comes home every Saturday evening just in time to have a terrible hitting, throwing row with his wife as K. and I are issuing out in gala mood to town. The children scream with fright and run outside to watch the parent drama from safety. The worst part is the eight children crying. The flying scrubbing-brush and the flapping broom are merely exciting. But I do feel for the woman. I said to the grandmother when she was discussing all this with me, "I'm on the wom-

an's side. Right or wrong, I'm always on the woman's side."

"He goes with other women, Moana doesn't like that."

"Neither would I like it."

"I wouldn't either."

Every Saturday night I say to K., "There's going to be a murder over there one of these Saturdays."

A rainy Thursday. What I appreciate about being in the infant room is that if there is anything wonderful coming up through the school the discovery is for me. My score so far is two brilliant minds, Reremoana and Tame Tuhi. Both Maoris with no white blood. I said to the Senior Inspector, "I want you to meet Reremoana and Tame. My two Ngarimu Scholarship candidates in seven years' time. In case I'm not here then."

Polly is practising at the piano. Her work is plaintive and true. There's more music in her composition than flesh and blood. The famous radio star, Kahu, is her uncle. Polly is mine. She is Mere's sister and has no mother. Mere told me, "My mother died on the 'randah." The Store people said, "Oh, Polly's mother? She died over the last baby." I'm very proud of my Polly and Mere. They're pretty, too, and blazing with something . . . pull, personality, or plus.

Yesterday, however, Mere and white June rubbed red chalk on their faces. It was a wet Wednesday. I had some seniors in, knitting, pocketing and practising orchestra work for the hour of dancing on break-up day. On top of the infant room. So when I saw these two running about laughing with this red on their faces something

111

snapped in my carefully built up patience. I said, "Wash your faces, then I'll speak to you."

Mere took this with the large carton of salt that she knew went with it . . . with such a statement. But white June didn't know about the salt. She broke into hysterical crying and trembling. I said amazed, "Don't cry! I won't growl!" But she was too far gone. She was possessed. "Don't growl at me!" she pleaded, clinging to me. There was only one thing to do. I picked her up and wiped her tears. At once she was comforted. But one or two of the seniors laughed. "Don't laugh!" I reproved. "Be kind!"

I have to special June. She has no little white girl companions in the infant room so I am that companion. We share pencils, blackboards and rubbers and I answer ten thousand questions and observations a day.

Epilogue: I was awake until about four in the morning over the June incident.

Waiwini, the queen of communication, is the piano find of the year. Her fingers are as pliant and willing as her nature. She has amazed me on the keyboard! Six. But where is the future for these three gifted Maoris, Reremoana, Tame and Waiwini? What future anyway? The Pakeha struggle for success? Better if they had none then. Let their brains and abilities increase the intensity and the quality of their communication. Their talking, their doorstep sitting and their loving . . . and their quarrelling. . . .

Mrs. Cutter, white Mark's mother, sent me flowers. *Score!*

Thrill of the week:
My Maori piano group playing with the orchestra. Thrill of the year really. Now I am freed from the keyboard and can conduct from the outside. *How* different!

I talk to them all day. I answer thousands and thousands of questions. Mainly they teach themselves. More and more I think that my converse with them is the main consideration. I have a very high standard of written composition.

112

But often the noise is too much at my age. And this particular brand of discipline. There's discipline all right. But it's the inner, instinctive discipline that obliterates the external, the imposed brand.

But oh, life is so appallingly short. I hope I have the courage to run a real infant seedbed, allowing the marvellously abstract pattern of behaviour that pushes up from the unconscious. When I'm rocking in my armchair at ninety and looking back I'll never forgive myself if I haven't used this time. Think of the regret that old age *could* be! To review the past and perceive what you *could* have done! Had you the courage!

I'm not going to Kahu's birthday party tonight. I'm too weary from the night lost over the white June incident.

A rainy Thursday . . . very . . . very . . .

My seven-year-old twins are singing at Kahu's coming-of-age tonight in the Assembly Hall in Hastings. They have already broadcast and appeared in the papers and are acquiring a fame. This morning when I asked them to give us their item in advance they picked up a ukulele and played it and sang to it in a way that staggered even me, used as I am to the gifts of this tribe.

The music in the blood of this pa! Conversely there is nothing constructive. They build nothing. Even the precious Meeting House is borrowed from Wairoa. They concern themselves only with the closest mediums of communication: talking, sitting, singing, dancing, drinking and loving: In all of which they attain no mean heights.

Note: They're notorious as the worst quarrellers since the migration.

Post-Holiday Notes

On the Friday before we broke up two detectives came to question three of our wild boys for breaking into the shop over the bridge, the Ice-Cream Shop, and stealing twenty pounds in different lots. One detective said to a *brother* of the suspected.

"Had any chocolate lately, Ted? Any chewing gum?"

"No." Guiltily.

"What? Didn't you get any?"

"I only had a little. They had it all." And so on. And there was the sleuthing over in ten or so words.

While these light proceedings were going on in the porch the Health Inspector came to see why we were applying for showers and laundry. Coming in the gate he tripped over a cat which had just that minute died there and brought it in by the tail. . . .

I get a vast amusement from the Police Court's counter campaign in the paper. Here am I assiduously trying to reinstate the school socially by putting everything we do in the paper, and regularly at the bottom of the page in small letters the police put something of a different quality in. Breaking and entering and thieving or the case of Pai's father who told the court that even his hardest thrashing would not get Pai to school. . . . I laugh aloud at the contemplation of all this. I wonder how many are sharing this joke with me.

Arriving at school this morning after the May break I was thunderstruck to find the most wonderful brown winter uniforms. Some of them had completed their pockets! Well at least I have always allowed for miracles in everyday life. Up they pop regularly. If only Mr. B. could see this. Culled from all over the place. From Napier to Wellington.

Moreover there is this delicate adjustment of staffing rules standing on my doorstep. In the person of a junior. A special dispensation, yes, but practical imagination too. But then imagination does not often get away itself without breaking some rule or other or paying in some way or other.

What a much better, much easier, much more accomplished day I had! Praise God and Mr. Tremaine!

Fernhill School
May 22nd

Re the Fernhill School Uniform:

DEAR MR. B.,

After the setback of a month or so ago when I was told that your firm would not handle the dark brown winter tunics and blazers I lost heart temporarily in these negotiations. However, since then, I have been amazed to find these uniforms appearing in the school in no mean numbers, obtained from sources ranging from Napier as far as Wellington, so I have found heart again.

Knowing the Maoris, as you must, at least as well as I do, you will recall how fond they are of clothes, especially uniforms. You will realise too the good effect a careful uniform has on the behaviour of a school. And although I have nothing (serious) to be ashamed of where the girls are concerned, nevertheless everyone knows that we have a few wild boys here, and from this point of view a good and carefully chosen uniform has an importance over and above appearance.

Would you kindly continue your efforts to arrange a supply of boys' uniforms, of the design and colours discussed? May I have a sample of trousers, shirt and blazer?

Also, will you still watch for a suitable brown print to preserve the continuity of the girls' summer outfits?

Thank you for your service and courtesy in the past. I understand perfectly your position where the handling of the winter tunics and blazers was concerned.

Yours faithfully,
S. HENDERSON (Mrs.)

I was amazed to find the Senior Inspector over at school the other day—Mr. Tremaine. I was delighted, too. He's a man of sympathy, that wonderful rare quality. Also very clever. I greeted him very warmly in the porch of the main building where I had gone over to see the doctor and nurse who were doing the school! "It's very nice to see you!" I said, thoroughly off guard.

"It's very nice to be here!" he said.

Then I ran off to the infant room.

But as the children came pouring in, in the design of flowing water, he was in the stream too! Matawhero had brought his black kitten to school and had put him on my shoulder. And as I looked up to him (he is very tall), I had to look across a loudly purring black kitten, sweeping his tail to and fro across my face. The children all grouped around us in their inimitable way, eyes agog, laughing at the kitten. . . .

"I've got a typewriter, Mrs. Henderson, that types in the printing you want. I can get my typist to do your books for you now."

"Where did you get it!" I cried almost hysterically.

Why the hysterics? No one can know the time and effort I have put into the hand-printing of my sixty Maori primer readers. So he spent until eleven o'clock going over my Maori primers with me. And now my books are going ahead. He said, "I've always felt that there was a bridge needed between the pa environment and the school. I believe you have something here."

It did please me to see him handling my poor little books, although the third edition is not poor. Again he wished to take one with him as a model but I squirmed out of it and promised to provide him with a model adequate enough for his typist. He and the secretary came in one day to see these books and the secretary said,

"May I take one with me?"

I said smartly, "Mr. Henderson never lets them leave the school!" Neither of them had an answer to this. And the secretary didn't speak to me again. So here was Mr. Tremaine saying the same thing but he didn't get a book.

I myself just can't get on any further with the third edition. As I told Mr. Tremaine, "I just can't do any more. I can make one model of each but can't multiply them. My printing is going off. I'm getting old! I'm getting on! I'm worked out! I'm fused!"

But everything is changed now. Mr. Tremaine is seeing to the printing, and I have an eye on a young man to copy my drawings. I said, "Congratulations, Mr. Tremaine, on rescuing this from its deathbed!" The years of experiment and ardour and invention I have poured on this idea of a Maori primer reader!

Note to Mr. Tremaine:

About those nouns with which I introduce the Ihaka books. I am constrained to question Mr. Schonnell's observation that we think in sentences. That's incomplete. We think in sentences but we see in single images. Particularly a Maori. A Maori child notoriously speaks in what I call "one-worders." But from one Maori to another these one-worders *are* complete sentences. For the Maori mind is essentially artistic in character. I mean that besides being powerful in imagery it is chaotic in operation. An image is represented by a single spoken word but its associated meaning is supplied by expression, gesture, intonation, cadence and, above all, *touch*. All of which is understood with consummate ease between one Maori and another since the Maori communal mind is not yet

broken up. Sympathy, in the more delicate sense of the word, is still almost on the level of telepathy with them. Word conversation quickly fades before sympathy, before gesture, expression and touch. I mean, verbal conversation gives way to sensual and physical conversation. Between intimates it dwindles to a minimum. To one-worders. . . .

The Maori language is known to be a flowery one but that is kept for oratory. A Maori child runs in to you and cries, "Man! Man!" And you read from his excitement, his drawing close to you, from his voice and from his hands pulling at you, "There's a strange man coming in the gate! I've never seen him before! Who is he? What does he want? Do find out all about him and tell me! I'm dying to know! I love exciting strangers coming here!"

I picked up a receiver once to get the exchange and overheard a complete conversation between one Maori man and another.

First man: Plough?

Second man: No!

And the intonations, the pauses, and the clicks of the receivers told everything else.

These nouns I introduce first are the one-word sentences of a Maori. And as such are indispensable in the transition from one intellectual climate to another. A Maori primer child can assimilate a noun with five times the speed he can a preposition or a pronoun. And ten times the speed if that noun is of emotional significance to him. And it is during his apprehension of these nouns that he incidentally becomes familiar with the letters and their ways so that by the time he reaches Book One with its *several-word* sentences he is more happily equipped to tackle pronouns, prepositions, verbs and conjunctions.

So I need these one-worders first. The thing is to choose them carefully. It is all part of the effort to relate the first Maori reading to the temper of the pa.

This design comes naturally to a Maori child . . . and to me.

Afterthoughts of Mr. Tremaine's visit to me:

Waiwini, the queen of communication, stood at the table the whole time, wholly given up to the study of our faces and expressions. I didn't send her away to do her work. I knew. I understood her lovely gift of understanding and sympathy even though she is only six. I can still see her face, leaning on an elbow, the ribbons on her hair jaunty and her large brown eyes completely open, completely absorbed in the play before her. I know why she was pulled there. She felt my emotion. Maoris can sense it. She couldn't possibly understand our conversation—our *verbal* conversation—but she understood with consumate ease my facial expression, my voice, my hands and my actions. She stood there from nine until eleven, until her head resting on her hand began to droop, but I knew that she was learning something much more important than the reading lesson she was scheduled to be doing. She shared with me every shade of passion that swung me about over the books . . . I knew it. I know Maoris. And I won't forget it.

During this Mr. Tremaine said, "I got this from a friend of mine." The wonderful typewriter he was referring to, that typed infant-room book printing. "I asked him to sell it to me, but it had been left him by a friend who had died. He wanted to still own it for sentimental reasons. It's the only one I know of in New Zealand. You're sure it's what you want? Of course he is only lending it to me."

I flung out my hand, like Mamma, at the sample of printing he had brought. "I could weep over that!" Then I ran to the storeroom and brought out the books I had printed by hand. One lot, two lots, then I brought them faster and poured them all over the table, heaps and heaps of them . . . more and more of them until he groaned and covered his eyes with his hands. . . .

Matawhero, as could have been predicted from the sensitivity of his composition, reacted with violence to the presence of my new junior. He embarked on a crescendo of showing off that gained in precariousness until the other afternoon when I was out coaching the senior Basketball and had left the infant room to Colleen, he struck Gordon, one of my white twin boys. I returned just in time to find Gordon possessed with sobs.

"What's the matter, Gordon?"

He tried to speak but couldn't. His twin brother said, "Matawhero hit him!"

This was no surprise of course but something racial began to boil in me, deep down, that the brown should strike the white. I read the danger in the threat of temper and said over-quietly, "You stay behind, Matawhero."

"He—he punched me in the stomach!" Matawhero improvised easily. But the idea of Gordon punching anybody or anything or in any other way displaying the presence of passion in himself was inorganic. I took no notice whatever. I comforted Gordon and left the matter temporarily to recover my temper.

The room had several of my big senior girls about, some cleaning and others at the piano and their knitting, also Colleen. After a while, when the infants had been dismissed, I said quietly to Matawhero, "You go now, Matawhero."

I can only put down what followed to the fact that he cares for me and felt my disapproval. Again in his passionate Maori way he reacted, especially with the stimulus of an audience, which he always appreciated. He stamped across the room, thumping his little feet and shaking his fist.

This staggered me! But before I could work it out and take his side with logic as I have trained myself to do, the boiling within burst up again. Very quietly I spoke to him. "Don't be cheeky, Matawhero."

But he must have read the threat in my voice with the instinct to read beyond words, the instinct to interpret anything emotional, as Maoris have. He was understandably hurt. He stamped his feet more frantically and waved his little fist, always of course with appreciation of his audience.

I was aware of the audience too. But in another way. I was very ashamed that they should witness such defiance. The temper, rising rapidly, won. But I wouldn't touch him myself, knowing my own temper. I thought of something less dangerous. "You go over to Mr. Henderson, Matawhero." Still quietly. I crossed the room and took his arm. But by the time we got to the outer step he sat down and broke down in loud crying. This was the worst part. I had asked him to do something he couldn't possibly do. I put my rage aside and began comforting him. "Don't cry," I said, patting his leg. "You're all right.

Where's your handkerchief?"

"Inside!" He scattered back into the room. Of course he didn't return, so I followed in. "Where's that boy?" I said.

There was the poor little thing over in the corner of the room at his desk taking a long time to get his handkerchief. "He's getting his handkerchief!" someone said defensively. I hadn't realised until then that of course they would all be on Matawhero's side. So I walked up to him. I knew I was wrong. Everything had taken a wrong turning the moment I had lost my temper. Well I would pay for my mistake. In front of them all. "You go home, Matawhero," I said, "but don't come back tomorrow. I won't have boys here who hit the others."

"I won't go home! I'm going to wait for Emily!"

Everything went then. But in time I realised that I mustn't touch him in a rage. I changed my mind. "You're going to Mr. Henderson," I said. "Get Mr. Henderson," I said to Waiwini. What an errand to ask what a person! She went off at a snail's pace, fiddling with her fingers. As for me, I took Matawhero by the back of the jersey and led him out the door, down the steps and a short way across the grass towards the main building. To the accompaniment of his protest, "I don't want to go home! I'm going to wait for Emily!"

Across the grass, however, he stopped. I still held him. Why was K. so long? I'd had enough of this drama. It began to rain, but I held him. Then he, the great Matawhero, changed *his* mind. "I'll go home," he conceded.

I looked round for someone else to get K. Waiwini had obviously lost her way in Matawhero's interests. I saw Gordon. A1! Who better? "Gordon, go and tell Mr. Henderson I want him." And off ran Gordon on this most joyous errand.

Down came the rain in torrents! There was a real gallery on the steps of the infant room now, including Colleen, for whom for three days I had been a model teacher. There were boys in the shed and on the steps of the main building, all watching by now. But I still held Mr. Matawhero Materina. At last K. appeared walking through the rain. "I want you to speak to this boy," I said. "He's been very naughty all day and very rude to me!" And handed him over. . . .

It doesn't please me to write this and I'm glad it is done. I'm very very ashamed. I know where I went wrong. When I lost my temper. . . .

I have been two days in Gisborne attending the High School Opera. When I was away Marion and Rangi slipped over to the house and cleaned it from front to back—washed the bathroom and kitchen. It was like a new pin—every bed, every room and even my notorious dressing table. Even the Boys' Room, which is usually quite beyond terminology, was done!

About Matawhero again. D. H. Lawrence said, "If a child annoys you, smack it and smack it hard. In its own interests. It must learn when it is annoying others." But then D. H. didn't have any children himself, which may be, conversely, why he had a clearer view than the rest of us. So tied up we get with our children! Then again a neurologist I know said, "These young two-year-olds coming into the world, throwing their weight about! It's a smack they want! Any other reproof breeds brooding. A smack at the right time, carrying with it its association." Personally, with my own sons, I have found that *only* a thrashing would make them get the wood.

Nevertheless . . . I still feel that Matawhero had as much right to his rage as I did. After all, here I am passionately cultivating the abstract, organic pattern of behaviour, yet here, at its most vital point, I deny it. Why? Pride, pride!

Disgusting! Simply disgusting!

Strangely I didn't have a four o'clock night over that. Maybe because I talked it all over twice. Once with Tom and once with K.

No one knows what I meet with here among the girls in the way of sulks, temper, temperament and tears. Boys too, for that matter. It all depends on what standard one uses to assess their behaviour whether or not it is worth it. European standards would prove their ways appalling. But from the Maori standard it is normal and comely enough. On the basketball field:

"Mrs. Heneson, may I change places with Paulette?"

"No."

Tears!

From someone: "Helen you're a cheat!"

Tears! And sulks for the rest of the game.

"Mrs. H., I want to play goal. I'm sick of playing center."

"You can't change your position until you know it perfectly. You still move your feet with the ball."

Rage! Head-tossing and so on. While the others observe full of sympathy and admiration.

I talked to K. about this and asked him for a formula for a sulky girl. He said, "Send her off at once and ignore her. Replace her."

Result: "Mrs. H., can I change with Rangi?"

"No."

Tears! Sulks!

"Right. Go. You're finished."

"No, no! I'm all right Mrs. H.!"

Simple.

But I'd never say "Don't cry." It's not the crying. I like the tears as much as they do. It's the sulks that spoil the game for everyone else. The tears are lovely. You know that they would be ready to flow for you too at a moment's notice, if the occasion arose.

As for the infant room, I could not consider a day's work complete without an outburst somewhere. And it all goes towards that feeling of relaxation in the room that ultimately will bring out the very best work they are capable of. And tears and temperament are a small price to pay for it. If it can be called a price.

I sent a batch of sixty prepared pages of my first Maori primer, Ihaka Book One, to Mr. Tremaine, whose office girl is to type the printing with this marvellous typewriter that types big, infant-room printing. I was so happy when I got them back.

I do the first picture on the page above the printing, then give my junior, Colleen, a carbon copy of the outline on the other five pages (we're making six of each) and all she has to do is to paint in the colour, which she does competently. So the books are creeping slowly ahead. I can't get over it myself. But I've always allowed for miracles in everyday life. *I expect* them!

The other day in walked a group of impromptu visitors from the board.

They said, "All of us at once!"

"I like you all at once. I like surprises."

"We couldn't go by without coming to see you."

"We'll be getting to know you all yet."

Marion was practising on the piano and was playing "Big Enough for Two." The whole room, who happened to be drawing at the time, at the wall blackboards and at their tables, joined in lustily. It gave me an idea. I said, "Would you like to see some primer hula?"

"I'd be delighted!"

So I ran to the piano, as with a junior I am never tired these days and run everywhere, and took over and began to warm the children up in my customary way, with a song or two first. "If I knew you were coming I'd have baked a cake!" and so on. They turned in their casual way and sang it from where they chanced to be. Then I slipped into the hula tune: "Just a little hula hula, hey, ha hey! . . ." and in no time there they all were, some clapping the rhythm, some singing the words, and the artists completely lost in the hula. You should have seen brown Jenny's hands! And Makere's fat little body, and Reremoana's rolling eyes! But the star was missing. Where was Waiwini? But Waiwini was far too much of a real star not to know when not to be there. She had to be

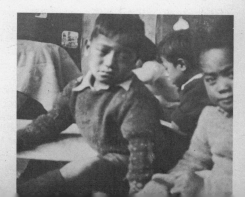

missed and then called. So I did. "Waiwini! Waiwini!"
And along came Waiwini in the best mobile hula, child
or adult, brown or white, I have ever seen; swinging herself up and down among the clapping singing children
who were converging in their delightful spontaneous way,
and swaying and gesticulating in a way that would have
satisfied anyone. . . .

It wasn't until well after they had gone that I wondered
whether or not that was quite the right thing to do in a
respectable Board infant room with such august visitors. . . .

However, "Act first and think last" is my motto.

We're all getting out and finishing our yellow pullovers
and gay school blazer pockets for the return match with
Twyford on Wednesday. For the first time on record in
twelve years I'll accompany the teams. I will that. I
haven't trained these three teams daily for nothing. I want
to *see*. I want to see their mistakes, to tell the truth, to get
on to them before Havelock North comes Friday week.
Ah, I'm getting cunning! Imagine me thinking in terms
of basketball!

Polly: "Mrs. Henderson, how old are you?"
"Why! ? !"
"It's my turn for the quiz this morning. It would do
for one of my questions."

Now Matawhero is the grandson of the Chairman of
the School Committee, of whom, I blush to say, I am not
wholly unaware as a woman. He is the biggest size I have
seen in men and Matawhero is the smallest. However they
meet on one thing. Lying. But I like lying. The imaginative
stuff, you know. Not the dull forseeable line.

The morning after the downfall of Matawhero, he came
to the school gate, then turned round and went home
again. I saw him as I was at the mirror in my bedroom.
And although it is a principle of mine never to run after
children (anybody for that matter), nevertheless, Matawhero was the grandson of the Chairman of whom I am
not entirely unaware of as a . . . what did I say last time?

I saw Matawhero returning reflectively homewards in

126

his sou'wester, oilskin and gumboots like Christopher Robin and called after him. "Matawhero! Come to school! You're all right!"

He turned and surveyed me with detachment. I felt scraggy-necked and old, like a witch, at his look. "Come back," I said on a lower and less confident key.

He thought this over for a moment, then turned on his way homeward.

Later when I was at school along comes a roaring bull —Mr. Chairman. "I was on my way to town! I met Matawherto coming home again! He said that he got a growling yesterday. He said that when he got to school this morning Mrs. Henderson sent him home and told him not to come back again!"

"That's only a child's tale, Peter," said K. the peacemaker. "Mrs. Henderson said no such thing."

"Well, that's what he told me! I was just going to get on the bus when I met him."

"But Peter, he's only a baby. Surely you're not going to go by the story of a baby."

"He said he got a growling yesterday."

"He did get a growling yesterday. He was very rude in the infant room and I gave him a piece of my mind."

Later the children called to me, "Peter's at the door!"

"Tell him to come in."

But he didn't come in as usual and said he wanted to

128

see Mrs. Henderson. So I went and looked at him over the heads of the very small ones making their houses with blocks. I was shocked to see how upset he was. He's well overweight and has a heart to boot. He held Matawhero's lunch. "I just wanted to see Matawhero," he said in his deep voice.

"He's here."

"I just wanted to give him his lunch."

I wondered why he hadn't just asked to see his grandson. Why call me? He still looked at me.

I said, "I'll call him."

I left him and called Matawhero. But that night it was his sad, helpless face (his wife is dead, you know) that I saw last thing before I went to sleep.

A few nights after that he was sitting in my drawing room after a Committee meeting. He sat very late, the only Maori habit he manifests when with us. "I'm very late," he admitted gruffly.

"Never mind. You can sleep late."

"Not me."

"Not you? Why not?"

"I've got to get my grandson's breakfast."

"Matawhero's? But what about his mother? Or his father?"

"It's my toast he likes. He says I get it just how he likes it. The toast his mother makes isn't just right."

A few days later the word "growling" was among the new ones to be learnt. From my Maori books of course. You'd never find a word like that in the respectable, ordinary, placid, monotonous, two-dimensional English books. Matawhero took one look at it and knew it for good.

Kahu came to school today at our request to prepare the children's Maori *waiata** and haka for the visit of Havelock North next week. He was dressed in the latest fashion and was dead on time at 2:30 P.M. I stayed in with his practice. I don't generally stay long as I can't stand the repetition of the simple tonic-dominant stuff they sing. But I did today, being free, with Colleen in the infant room.

* *waiata:* Maori song.

And this I found out: This incredible patience they display in singing a new song over and over again is due not wholly to their obsession with a new song but to the fact that it drugs. Very pleasantly too. The same tune, over and over again with its persuasive simple harmonies, combined with that particular indescribable quality in a Maori voice, drugged *me*. And I thought as I sat there singing to the Maori words on the blackboard with Kahu playing the guitar, "Here is a wonderful instance of the intact, communal Maori mind in operation. They sang as one person, with Kahu as the heart of that person, and with the rhythm of one person.

I had come in to endure the learning of this new song in order that when Kahu was not available I could at least keep the work going. But by staying I learnt that this idea was futile. I could never get out of them what Kahu got out of them.

Simply, I was not a Maori.

So I don't need to go to practice again.

Primer One Reading
Progress of February entrants

Harry (absent a great deal)	3 words
Patchy (whom we only just discovered to be deaf)	12 words
Blossom (protracted babyhood)	10 words
Wiki (just plain dull)	12 words
Mark (a normal European with good attendance)	46 words
Tame (a brilliant full Maori)	68 words

I have definitely decided to bring the Europeans up on the English books, and Maoris on the Ihaka Maori books. It makes twice the number of divisions in the primers but there's no alternative. The white children love the white book and the brown children love the brown book. They say so, although there is enough telling evidence without their saying so.

I think that the earlier an actual *book* is put into their hands the speedier the vocabulary increases. The feel of the pages, the turning them over and the meaning in the pictures all provides an impetus. I've only just put the

first Ihaka books into the hands of the brown children, since they were not ready until now. But I expect an increase . . . a word increase from now on that is better than that to date.

I'm sorry to have to note that I think that Mark would have had a larger vocabulary if I had begun him on the white books instead of the brown books and had let him handle a book earlier.

The A team sat on the mat in the infant room at playtime. Quiet and serene. I don't know why.

"I'm sorry," I said, "to have to punish Helen—" Helen, loudmouthed and confident, suddenly lurched backward and red spread in a rush over her face—"for bad behaviour at Twyford. For sulks and disobedience. On account of her sulks you didn't score at all in the second half and almost lost the game. A girl can cry. We all cry when we're upset. You can forget your place in the game. That's all right too. You can learn it again. But sulks, no! You will stand down for the Havelock game, Helen. I would put you out for good except that you've been a good girl this year. A very good girl and have helped me a lot. On account of that I'll give you another chance. I'll let you play in the Paki Paki game and see how you behave then."

131

I had been very nervous before this, thinking that Helen would turn on me with her loud, long tongue. I didn't dream of such a complete collapse from the opposition.

In the passing game I was teaching the B, Jane Hammond stopped since she was not getting the best of it. Hammonds insist on the best coming their way. I tried to ignore the still, sulky figure, hoping she would recover and spare me a scene. But Lily cried out, "Jane, you're not playing!" So I had to blow the whistle and see it.

"You go inside. You're sulking."

The Hammond baby tried attack, and the habitual loud mouth. She burst into loud crying and railing at Lily, "You shouldn't speak to me like that! What a way to speak to me! To say things like that to me!" It was an obvious copy of rows in the pa. Lily had not said anything beyond the observation that she was not playing.

"Go inside. You've stopped playing. And I won't have sulks."

Not a move from the Hammond. Louder railing, more hysterical crying still and spinning tears.

"Go inside."

Jane still played the attack.

"Lotus, go and get Mr. Henderson please."

The attack of tears and accusations rose to a climax as K. came down the steps.

"Mr. Henderson, here is a girl sulking."

"You shouldn't speak to me like that, Lily! What a way . . . !"

K. said, "Go inside."

The Hammond baby for once didn't get her own way. She went inside smartly. As for us we went on with the game.

"Hands up who are doing knitting." I was visiting K.'s senior room.

A few hands went up. One or two smelt trouble in time and knew better. The Hammonds to be exact.

"Where's your knitting, Winnie?"

"At home, Mrs. Henderson."

"Where's yours, Jean?"

"At home, Mrs. Henderson."

Ronda lost interest and picked up a book and began reading.

"Don't," said K.; "read a book when Mrs. Henderson is speaking." He called her out and gave her a very bad growling at. She took it all right though. Maoris have a hard skin. Many of them. And in any case are accustomed to being growled at. It's one of the few respects they have. I went on. I was sickening for a cold and wholly fed up.

"Where's your knitting, Helen?"

"I was knitting out on the basketball field and one of the boys ran into me and broke my needle."

"Where is it?"

"At home, Mrs. Henderson."

"You've got knitting, Rachel. Why don't you put up your hand?" Slowly the hand went up.

"Where is it?"

"It's at home, Mrs. Henderson."

"Where's yours, Ronda?"

"At home."

"Where's yours, Netta?"

"At school, Mrs. Henderson."

I turned to the man beside me who was no longer my

husband but my headmaster. "Mr. Henderson, these girls know that there is knitting every day at two thirty. But they very seldom come and don't bring their work to school. Some of them began before the May holidays. No one has finished yet. I want you to speak to everyone who does not bring her knitting at two thirty."

"I most certainly will!" Down went all their names.

I felt my temper going and tried to read the danger signals. I looked about the large crowded room of senior children. "The wool is provided. The needles are provided. The time is arranged. And over there is a teacher who knows all about knitting. And you still can't do your knitting. Not one girl has finished a pullover on her own. You're—" I sought for the word that I knew from long experience over the years would hit them the hardest— "you're just . . . *dunces!*"

Things however were also "just anyhow" in my own mental climate. Soon I would have to stop.

"This knitting is to be completed by Friday. Otherwise there will be more than a talking to." But my voice had begun to quaver. My temper had gone. So I went too.

I broke my appointment with the A team for practice for the encounter with Havelock on Friday and went home. There, to somehow cheer myself up, I went through the cupboards, and, in spite of the diet I maintain to counteract the unfair consequences of middle age, I ate everything that I fancied and made the tea. "Maori" I said to myself with all the racial prejudice in my voice that I had been trying to combat in others for years.

The sponge cake was good though. And so was that cold, crumbed cutlet. And as for the tea, with thick cream, ah! It lifted me to the realms of the immortals!

"Poor Maoris . . ."

The next morning, however, I said to K., who was once more Headmaster and not husband, "There were two girls who had begun knitting but who were too wise to put up their hands. Jane and Crystal Hammond."

So I didn't go to school today. I left the infant room to Colleen. When the Head came home to lunch he said mildly, in between the broth and the tea, "There's a lot of knitting at school today."

He's a wonderful headmaster.

However, this is not fiction but a diary—a record of reality. So although I don't enjoy it I must tell this. This morning I sent for the A captain. Marion.

"Marion. I told some of your girls to have their pullovers finished by Friday. But I don't think that is possible. Tell Della I will give her till next Wednesday. And Jane, she's so far behind I'll give her until next Friday week. Tell them that."

Whatever could that have been though that was to be "more than a talking to?"

I'm *very* impressed!

Well they're really wonderful children, otherwise I would never be bothered about them or write about them. Kahu has been up today, dead on time, and he took the action songs for Havelock's visit tomorrow. There's something coming there. I've never seen such likely material and *never* such an excellent teacher. Also the senior music is lovelier every day . . . you should hear Della play the "Harry Lime Theme" and Polly "The Umbrella Man" and George "Song at Twilight." And there's a lot of knitting just now. Lovely vivid yellow pullovers. And more winter uniforms in spite of B.'s never even answering my last letter.

STOP PRESS NEWS

Yesterday, while Havelock North was here in body and in bulk, who should pay me a visit but Mr. Lopdell and Mr. Tremaine, Senior Inspector of Primary Schools

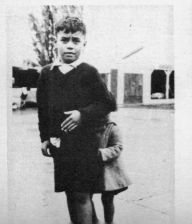

for New Zealand. To see my Maori primer books. They spent the afternoon with me, while my teams, in their brilliant yellow and their brand-new combination, fought out their battles without me.

Next week these men are bringing to the Fernhill School, to see my tender little books, the Director of Education. Thursday. I'm very nervous indeed. Mr. Tremaine has asked me to prepare a model set to take with him to Wellington on Monday week. I am doing that now.

So I'm on the *fourth edition*. Mr. Tremaine has asked for a set for himself. I replied, "You don't have to ask for that, Mr. Tremaine. That's been in my mind for some time."

"Thank you, Mrs. Henderson." He's very tall.

I haven't even got time to record all the interesting conversation. Except this.

"We'll bring the Director out here next week."

"No, no, don't bring the Director!"

"Oh, but he's a lovely man."

"I'm frightened of the Director."

"Have you met him?"

"No."

"There's nothing to be afraid about. He's a man who has respect for and who sees the importance of small things."

"I don't like being important."

Then I noticed that Mr. Tremaine had become silent, whereas in his plans and excitement over the Maori primers he had been like a ship in full sail. How I hate and fear the killing of inspiration! And that's what I was doing with my little objections. A rush of faith in this big tall man in grey suffused me. I clasped my hands and looked up into his face. "Mr. Tremaine. Whatever you *say*, I'll *do*."

"Thank you, Mrs. Henderson."

In town that night, last night, Friday, shopping with K., I saw a tall man in grey with hat and coat, I thought for a moment it was he. But it wasn't.

Praise God the Director didn't come. But Colleen and I got our room looking lovely. I said to her, "It takes a Director to get us to do our room."

I went into the Board's office on Monday to get that wonderful typewriter that does infant-room printing, in order to complete the Maori primer, Ihaka Book One, for Mr. Tremaine. He had to lend it to me or he wouldn't have got the primer for the Director. Making that Ihaka Book One on Saturday, Sunday and Monday with the marvellous typewriter, making it *for* someone, a demonstration copy, I spent three of the happiest days and nights of my life.

Helen, whom I stood down from the A team for the Havelock match for sulking, has not been to school since. "She said she's not going to play basketball any more, Mrs. Henderson, and she said she's not coming to school any more," the others told me. I laughed.

Colleen, taking my bigger ones for a walk to find the pussy willow, met Helen. She said, "I'm not coming back to school. My mother said."

Colleen, being little more than a schoolgirl herself, had the perfect answer. "Don't you want to play Central on Tuesday?"

"Are you playing Central on Tuesday?"

"Mrs. Henderson wants you to play defence on Tuesday."

"She'll have to get me there first."

It's lovely and peaceful without her though.

138

Both my teams won from Havelock on Friday. There was some fair combination.

The Inspectors were there and heard the action songs. Which were fair.

All this behaviour in the pa. This absence of the inner discipline. It's the abstract pattern of behaviour all right that I admire so much. Secretly. But my word it's not popular with the public. It makes me wonder what will happen next. Obedience? Not to *anyone!* The only time I see it is at school. And then not always. It's *amazing*.

My entries today I know are very disjointed but as long as they go in, never mind how. I'm still half exhausted after Director week. I put a pussy willow drawing on the board for the "Pussy Willow" song which takes standing. Hours. Little grey pussies with large pale green eyes crawling out from the buds and cavorting on the stalk, and falling off. And the three days, three nights span on that demonstration copy of the Ihaka Book One. Well.

Tonight we are having a film evening in the drawing room with the new projector which we bought from our Gala Day. Now this projector is just about the most wonderful thing that has appeared in my life lately, run a close second by this marvellous typewriter of Mr. Tremaine's that prints infant-room printing. We're having some of our hardest-working parents along, and Peter, the chairman. To sit in my own drawing room by the fire and see these films from all over the world is almost more than I can contain. No chewing-gum gangs in the back seat. No cheeky flappers talking through the drama and no ice-cream cones crackling in the tender opening scenes and no cold drive home afterwards is too much joy for fastidious, touchy me. Ah, it was worth all the work that Gala Day.

There's two and a half hours' worth tonight.

I'm tired these evenings. There has been an influx of five-year-old Maori boys. Only infant mistresses who have handled these will know why I am tired these evenings. Their boots weigh a ton each, their attention span is about ten minutes, their voices are like wild bulls', and to teach them is a simply fantastic performance. For weeks

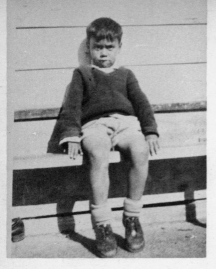

you teach them to obey, the actual teaching being small. They are the only real clue we have to what a Maori warrior was really like in the past, in this stage before the European discipline is clamped down on them. Of course they are not *all* in this category. But what with Waiwini's brother, Matawhero's brother, Leila's brother, Puia's son and Babe's cousin, also baby Betty, and tiny wee Mardi, and did I leave out the Tamati baby, Larry? That Tamati baby Larry!

Babe's cousin is called Seven. I had barely sent these little ones out early when in backfires Patchy.

"Mrs. Hen'son, Seven punched me in the stomach."

"Well, stay in here with me."

Waiwini's brother screams from the playground in true Waiwini style.

"Polly," I say to Polly who is in here making the blazer for which I bought the stuff, "go out and see to that."

"It's Waiwini's brother, Mrs. Henderson; Seven hit him with a stick."

Pammy runs in. "Mrs. Hen'son, Matawhero's brother is fighting Babe's cousin, Seven."

"Good."

In comes Bruce with the axe. "Mrs. Henderson, can I leave the axe in here? Seven is trying to chop Wi."

140

"Yes, just tuck the axe in behind the door. Colleen, please go out and bring in our relations."

Matawhero and his brother both appeared in bright green blazers. Matawhero, who knows that the uniform is brown and yellow, was embarrassed. However he and his grandfather the Chairman are hard to corner. "Mrs. Hen'son," said he brightly, "what say we change the uniform to green?"

Helen hurried to school on Monday and ran into Colleen. "Miss Burns, am I still to play Central on Tuesday?"

Score for me and Colleen. However the Central game is postponed and we face on Friday the formidable winners of last year's competitions: *Paki Paki!* You should have seen the shiver that went through the lines when K. told them this morning! This is our Waterloo, I'm afraid. I had hoped to have many practice games before we met these people but there have not been many. True we have won them all but these are very big children. Only technique, combination and tricks will beat them. And speed. My A team is coming on but . . . I've got a weak point in the center. I'm glad to have Helen back for this battle. K. had a talk with her this morning. I don't know what he said but she is quite tame now, obedient and quiet. Unrecognisable.

I saw Aroha in town yesterday. She looked like a flower from a Paris boulevard. She's fair for a Maori. She looked exquisitely beautiful, obviously pregnant, and well dressed. Our thirteen-year-old schoolgirl. On one side was a woman wheeling a pram, possibly her mother, and on the other a handsome young Maori. Presumably the son-in-law. That's how some people do it. Work that out.

"I defy you," I said to Colleen this afternoon, "to take our relations for a lesson."

"What shall I teach them?" she asked with all the gaiety and confidence of youth . . . of sixteen.

"All the letters that are in 'house' and 'truck' and 'Daddy.' That gang nearly killed me yesterday, you know. I thought last night, I'll put Colleen on to the relations tomorrow. Now I'm going to time you, Colleen."

The bell had gone a few minutes ago but the relations

had ignored it. Colleen looked at the clock. "It's nearly twenty past two."

"Aha! That's just it! The bell went at ten past! Where are they? And it's cheating to go and get them."

Colleen was not in the least bewildered. "Rangi," she said to one of the slower of my five-year-olds, "go and get all those other Little Ones. Tell them they are to come in for a lesson."

Rangi doesn't know what "lesson" means and has limited English. Moreover I've seldom had any result from telling a child. However it was Colleen's dilemma and I said nothing. I laughed though. "It's nearly twenty past," I said.

Of course no children came in. So I said, "You can send one of those out for them." I pointed to Jean and Polly, who were in there sewing.

"Polly!" said Colleen, warming up, "Go and bring all the Little Ones. I want them for a lesson."

After a while, in their own time, they appeared, preceded by the crashing of boots and argument. Colleen was just about to seat them. "Their boots have to come off," I said, "and they have to get their own chalk and blackboards and dusters. And it's against the rules to do anything for them or say 'Don't.'" "Take all your boots off and come back and sit here! All you Little Ones!" she cried. "Get your blackboards and chalk and dusters!"

Then I sat back to thoroughly enjoy the next.

I did thoroughly enjoy the next. I laughed out loud many times. Colleen's voice rose with the challenge and she took a wonderful lesson for a sixteen-year-old. Everybody worked and she never once let go an impatient remark. "But," I reminded her, "I had Matawhero's brother yesterday. He's not here today."

"But Matawhero's brother does everything I tell him!"

"All right. But look at Babe's cousin. Seven. He's asleep! You must have been boring."

"I saw him yawning before he went to play. That wasn't me."

"That's so. I noticed that myself."

"Wi, wake up Seven."

"No! Don't wake up Seven!" I cried. "You'll never hear me complain at Seven asleep. I wish a few more of them

142

would drop off!"

"I've got through all the letters, Mrs. Henderson."

I looked at the clock. "Twenty minutes. Now you have to get their boots on again and their things put away and get them outside *this* window."

I never saw such action before. "Look, I'm going to put you on those relations, Colleen. I'll take the ladies and gentlemen."

"I'll time you tomorrow," she said.

I'm nervous about tomorrow. I have just remembered that she didn't have Waiwini's brother today either. "They've worked very well," she said.

"Of course I have trained them a bit."

You see. Waiwini's brother and Matawhero's brother will be here tomorrow and Babe's cousin will be awake. Ah, well. . . .

"Colleen, I'm going home now. I'm very tired. I've got that pa team coming up after school at half past four to play my A and B. You wind all this up."

There was Polly and her blazer to wind up, Lotus and her pocket, Frances was giving Netta a lesson on the piano, Reremoana and Edna were painting and the upper primers were writing a story. That's not counting Mark writing a letter to his aunties, and Patchy. . . .

I have arranged a hurried practice game with the youth club at the pa to brush up the match experience of my teams for Paki Paki. One day's notice is apparently enough. Preferable. I hope the boys they have chosen to play for them do not include the two Hawkes Bay reps, Kahu and Titi.

There's something wonderful in this youth club, even though Peter, the chairman, says that that's where all the sixteen-year-old unmarried mothers originate.

"What exactly is the purpose of this youth club?" I asked him.

"To get the young people together," he replied gruffly, way down behind his throat.

I thought of Gail Tamati crying over her sixteen-year-old marriage, Whareparita's twins in the cemetery and Aroha like a madonna in town yesterday.

"Together," I repeated after him.

For some time I have fancied myself a hermit, but after refereeing that game just now with the pa youth club team, I wonder. If that's not life I don't know what is. If it's not life I encounter in the melee of this Maori school . . . then what is life?

If life is absolute self-forgetfulness then I've just had half an hour of it.

For a start I had to fight for the whistle. Caroline had it and was determined to referee. I called this match especially for practice for Friday. To train my girls. I let her begin but I soon demanded it from her in as loud and as enthusiastic a voice as any of them. She sulked at once. And mumbled. But I carried on. The "couple of boys" they apologised for having to use turned out to be four men. Including Kahu, the Hawkes Bay rep. The score of course was about 9-2. Speed! I never saw such passing.

At half time Caroline came up to mumble officially. She said the rules were ragged. It's hardly ever I use an American expression but to myself I said, "I'll show them 'ragged'!" So the third half—we had three halves—no one got away with anything.

If you'd seen those boys jumping—men, I mean—jumping right *over* the girls!

I praised them afterwards. They were a lovely lot of Maori youth. How I pray the drink does not get hold of them! I don't mind if passion gets hold of them. But not drink.

Lovely strong, tall, quick, well-mannered, dignified young people they are. And good-looking.

I was just having that last little cup of tea before school to brace myself to meet the infant room when Paulette came to the door with this note from Jane.

"Dear Mrs. Henderson, I can't play Paki Paki today Mrs. Henderson because I've got double pneumonia."

I had had something from my private life on my mind before the knock on the door but after this I fell to thinking with concern of Jane's double pneumonia. The double pneumonia that I knew hadn't allowed careful letter-writing, but perhaps this was a different kind.

It was wet on Paki Paki day so at twelve K. rang and postponed the visit. However at one we were all petrified to see a large bus draw up at the gate in the rain. . . .

WE

BEAT

PAKI PAKI!

As I have said, this team of Paki Paki has never been beaten in history. They have always been the champions of the Hastings area.

Now my yellow jerseys are the champions of the Hastings area.

Dreams sometimes come true.

But not without something just like work.

After all the Paki Pakis had gone, the yellow team clustered round me, nine brown hands shook mine, nine brown faces glowed and nine brown voices congratulated me on my coaching. They said, *"Now* we know you are a good coach, Mrs. Henderson. *Now* we'll listen."

I was very happy.

And shopping in town that night everywhere I looked I saw yellow, and the heartache I had over something in

my private life was constantly defeated.

As a colour, I like yellow.

The reading is very much on my mind. All my other interests in the writing world are put aside until I satisfy myself on this matter. I am continuing experiments at school on the words of most vital meaning to a child to begin with. These words seem to be sorting themselves out with alarming clarity around the two main instincts, fear and sex.

I began to suspect this when I tried the word "kiss." The children, five-year-old Maoris, discussed it excitedly. They returned to the book to find the place once more and the next morning ran in early to tell us that they could still spell "kiss."

I took the hint and looked for a word to represent the first and strongest instinct, fear. But the only one I had was "frightened," which did not recommend itself as a first word on account of its length. Although I knew that it has always been an easy word to teach, and one that I have always used extensively. However, I tried it, and it won, even against "kiss," which is according to the importance of the two instincts. It was learnt immediately by the new entrants, and another thing occurred that I had not noticed before. An intelligent, new Maori, just five, repeated the word "frightened" over and over again to himself.

"Cried" was third.

In "frightened" and "cried" I feel that I have the two words for that side of nature, fear, representing cause and effect. Now, with "kiss" established I think there must be another word, stronger than "kiss," representing the cause on this side. It may be "love."

But I seldom hear them use "love." And have not tested it for that reason. I mean to test this word on Monday.

The slow readers among the February entrants have begun reading at last. Reading cards composed of these words.

Words still in the running: (The numbers indicate how many children out of the nine I had at the time recognised the words which I had in a list.)

First Test

football	3
hit	1
fight	1
kiss	7
cried	5
haka	6

Introduction of "frightened"

Second Test

kiss	7
haka	4
cried	5
frightened	9

TENTATIVE CONCLUSIONS

1. The verbs need to be presented in the past tense in order that simple sentences may be made without the need for extras; *e.g.*, to us "cry" would require "will" in "Rangi will cry." "Will is hard to learn and is to be left out. Therefore "Rangi cried." "Mummy kiss*ed* me," instead of "Mummy will kiss me."

2. With these most powerful words it is an obvious offence to provide pictures. The pictures are already there in the child's mind, individual, and emotionally equipped. I offer all these words *without* pictures.

3. "Come," "and," and "look," which begin the English books and on which the first two or three books are built, are probably among the weakest words in the language. To begin an infant reader on. The "Janet and John."

4. I've made a colossal mistake in following blindly the lead of the *allegedly* scientific English books, "Janet and John," in building my first Maori book, Ihaka Book One, on those words, "come" and "look" and "and." Never suspecting other than that good thinking had been put into the compilation of these readers.

5. How the Maori child *pays* for the mistakes of others. The one or two years lost to them in the Maori infant room echo at the top of the school when they reach Std. 6, Form II (or not) at the age of fourteen or fifteen, delaying their secondary education until they have lost heart and fall into trouble socially.

Here is the impromptu reading card on which one of my backward Maori five-year-olds at last learnt to read. He read it on sight, and by the lighting up of his face, he *understood*.

Daddy
Mummy

Ihaka
hit
cried
kiss
Daddy hit Ihaka.
Ihaka cried.
Mummy kissed Ihaka.
Daddy hit Ihaka.
Ihaka cried.
Kiss Ihaka Mummy.

Questioned on it he understood it. He has stalled for about six weeks on "Come," "and," "look."

"Mummy" may be one of the words.

Also "I" and "me."

Cards will be prepared built on these chosen words.

Verbs are sentences in themselves.

No pictures accompany them.

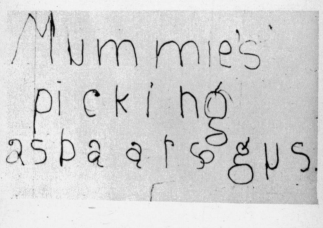

COMPOSITIONS

1. RITI

Hine said to
Me Look here.
She saw a cake then Rosie
hit us. mary
said the Kai is cooked
then she said
hurry up or you
will get late

150

2. MAKERE

> Mummy and Daddy
> took me to Wellington.
> I saw two policemen
> on the road. They
> had a accident on
> The road.

3. MATAWHERO

> Yesterday I came home
> late. My big brother
> gave me a hiding.
> Then I start to cry.
> Then I have to go to sleep.
> I'm sick of writing.
> That's all.

4. IRINI

> My father got
> drunk. and He drank all
> the beer by He self.
> and we had a party

These are my test children. By which I mean the children I hope will prove my belief that Maori children can do the infant room in two years and not three. K., who was in this afternoon, didn't think much of all their chances. Although Reremoana is ready now. And Waiwini nearly. However, there's half a year to go yet. It's the sentences they are just learning. They think that the full stop must come at the end of a line willy-nilly.

Rongo, the light-toed, of the "little bit dance," writes heavily on the blackboard for all to see,

> Mummy is crying
> because Daddy
> hit her in the face. Mummy is
> going to Nanny's today. Daddy is
> angry.

Rongo, exquisitely dressed and every silken black hair in place, writes on the paper I think I'd better give her,

> just because
> Daddy got wild
> and so I got
> wild because
> Daddy was drunk.
> Then he hit
> Rongo.

Rongo, whom I had been thinking the most adored child in Maoridom until she bought a book and pencil and rubber, writes,

> When I got
> up I got
> ready for school
> and I hurried
> because Daddy
> was wild
> and he looked
> cross.

I hate (writes white Dennis to himself in his little book)

> going
> up in the sky.
> When we die.

I hate the
sky because it
is too high.

I got a growling
last night
because my
sandals. were.
wet

Last night (writes my full Maori Tame, in wonderfully
controlled lettering)
I fell out Of
bed so Daddy Told
Mummy to
shiff over.

My Mummy (writes Irini Sung, who has an eye for
adult relationships)
is going to
the funeral with my
uncle. They went
on the 8 o'clock
bus. It is down at
Utapepi. I don't know
who died. She is
coming back
tomorrow. When
she comes back
she is going
to town to get some
meat.
Mummy said to Daddy
give me that money else I
will give you a hiding.
Daddy swear to Mummy.
Daddy gave the money
to Mummy. We had
a party. My father
drank all the beer by
hisself. he was drunk.
Mummy (writes Irini Sung in the exercise book I buy

for her myself since all the child allowance and the shearing money goes down in drink)

> gave me a hiding
> and told me to
> go and get the
> paper. so I got
> the paper and
> took it to Mummy.
> Then I told daddy
> that Mummy had
> the paper so
> daddy told me
> to go and get
> the paper.

"Mrs. Henderson, Seven's got a knife. He's cutting my
stomach."

"Colleen, please go and disarm Seven."

"Mrs. Henderson, I'm going to write a letter to Miss
Burns when I go to Health Camp."

"Waiwini! I thought it was I you were going to write
to!"

"I can't. Your name's too long."

"Mrs. Henderson, how do you spell 'boko'?"

"Why, what are you writing?"

"He donged me on the boko."

"Colleen, what *is* a boko?"

"Irini, have you brought your fourpence for your
pencil?"

"My mother she haven't got fourpen."

"And that, Colleen, is the home where eighty-four
pounds went at poker and drink last week. The child allowance for a big family and the big wool bonus. All the
child money."

"Mrs. Henderson, I'm sick of writing."

"Well, go and write, 'I'm sick of writing.' "

"Mrs. Henderson, you said I could play the piano
when we come in."

"That's right."

"Can I play it now?"

"Have you finished your writing?"

"No."

"Well, finish it. Then you can go to the piano."

"Really, Colleen, the things these children say I have said!"

"You do say a lot of them."

"Not all?"

"No, not all."

"You have heard me say things that I've denied after, then?"

"Oh yes!"

"It's my practise, Mrs. Henderson."

"Carry on then. Scales and arpeggios first."

"Mrs. Henderson, you said *I* could play the piano when I had finished my work."

"No I didn't."

"Yes you did, Mrs. Henderson."

"Did I, Colleen?"

"I heard you say that."

"All you Little Ones come here to me."

"Do you want this pussy willow or shall I put it out?"

"Mrs. Henderson, come and see my work on the blackboard behind the piano."

"Play those scales with both hands, Marion."

"You said I could paint this afternoon."

"That's right. Get your colours mixed."

"I haven't got any paper."

"I thought I told you to bring some paper?"

"Somebodies pinched it."

"Wrong fingering, Marion. One two three, then thumb."

"Betty's crying."

"What for? Jean, that seam is to be machined close to the edge."

"Seven put sand in her neck."

"Colleen, bring in Seven."

"What's this word?"

" 'Between.' "

" 'Atween'?"

" '*Be*tween.' I told you Little Ones to come here. Wiki. Blossom, bring those Little Ones to me."

"I can't find my pencil. . . ."

"Colleen, have you ever heard them make up something I didn't say?"

"Yes, sometimes."

"Somebodies taken my pencil."

"Don't say 'Somebody has taken my pencil.' Say 'I have lost my pencil.' "

"Who is the captain of the B team for the competitions, Mrs. Henderson?"

"I have lost my pencil."

"But I gave you one this morning."

"Who is the captain of the B team for the competitions, Mrs. Henderson?"

"I haven't picked one yet."

"You picked Hirani."

"I most certainly did not."

"Well who is?"

"I'll pick one later. Colleen, that seam of Jean's."

"I've lost my pencil."

"Good, Marion. That bass was right."

"Shall we nominate the captain?"

"No. I'll do all the picking of the captains. I'll pick someone who has been regular at practise and who hasn't sulked."

"You picked Hirani."

"I haven't picked any captains for the competitions. Did I, Colleen?"

"You picked Hirani."

"Here's Seven, Mrs. Henderson."

"Not really!"

"I heard you pick Hirani."

"What's Seven here for?"

"I've got no pencil, Mrs. Henderson."

"Who can lend Irini a pencil?"

"Here, Irini."

"Who is the A captain for the competitions?"

"Why can't you wait until I pick one?"

"Mr. Henderson wants to know now so he can send in the entries."

"That's the family, Colleen, who can't afford fourpence for a pencil but put eighty-four pounds down the drain in the weekend."

"Can I play the piano now Mrs. Henderson? I've finished my work."

"Who is the A captain Mrs. Henderson?"

"Here's Seven Mrs. Henderson."

"Will you write me some new music Mrs. Henderson?"

"Betty's crying Mrs. Henderson."

"This pencil is broken Mrs. Henderson."

"I've got my paints mixed Mrs. Henderson. But I've got no paper."

"Now all you Little Ones get a blackboard and chalk and duster and come to me. Come and sit on the mat. . . ."

"Aren't you coming to see my work behind the blackboard?"

"What shall I do with this pussy willow? Mrs. Henderson?"

"Mrs. Henderson?"

"Mrs. Henderson?"

"Colleen," I told Mr. Lopdell and Mr. Tremaine when they were out here recently, "supplies the common sense in the infant room. That's all we were short of over there. Real sense. Now we're quite balanced."

"And what do you supply?" one of them asked.

God! Here was my reputation in the hands of a sixteen-year-old! I turned to her, my hands clasped. "Colleen," I pleaded, "what do I supply?"

Colleen is tall. She thought a moment from her height while the men and I waited.

"Oh," she said with the confidence and gaiety of adolescence, "she supplies the patience!"

Peter, the chairman and Matawhero's grandfather and an intellectual, came in for a cup of tea after school yesterday. He seemed tired. He's a man of about sixteen stone, bald and sixty-five. One of the best of the best Maoris. A man of principle and a man of the church.

"How are you?" I asked, concerned.

"Ready for the corner." The churchyard is at the corner. "Why?"

"I've got no energy."

"What did the doctor say last time?"

"I haven't been for about three weeks."

"Don't you feel well, Mr. Materina?"

"It's this cold I can't get rid of."

"It's a strange thing," I said to K., "that he shouldn't have more resistance to a cold, when he's on such a strict diet."

"Why don't you eat potatoes, Peter?" said K.

"You're short on inspiration," I said. "You haven't been to see us often enough."

"I came last Sunday and you were all at work."

"Every day, nevertheless, is my sabbath."

"I'm ready for the corner. I haven't even got the strength to dig my own hole. But I daresay a bit of kerosene on the stack of wood at home would do. With me on top."

I poured him a very, very special cup of tea.

Mark Cutter is on my mind. He's home. His mother, who hates us all, won't buy him his new book, complaining that he is going too quickly. There is something seriously wrong with my reading methods after all. I was stung at the criticism and when it came time to teach writing I didn't give Mark a pencil and paper, saying that his mother would say he was going too fast. "You keep to the blackboard and chalk, Mark." Tame had pencil and paper beside him.

"I'll ask my mother," he begged. "She might buy me one."

"She might not."

He was deeply upset. I comforted him. He cheered up. But he's not here today. I'm very uneasy and deeply ashamed. I'm an appalling teacher. After lunch that day

I had planned to say to Mark when I got back, "Your mother is right, Mark. It's best not to have a new book." Just to save him the pain of division between his mother and me. But I forgot. Dear little Mark.

"Helen, I want you to have your brown skirt to go to town to the basketball competitions next week. Either buy one or make one or borrow one. I want all my children to be in brown next week."

In two years there has never been a thing bought for Helen. And the uniform has been ignored.

"Colleen, please tell Mr. Henderson that I can no longer spare you from one to two. Not until we have tamed the relations."

"Dear," I said to the Head over lunch, "do you think you could keep the axe shut away?"
"The axe!"
"Seven chops the others."
"Mrs. Henderson, Seven's trying to kill us with the axe!"
"Colleen! Axe! Seven!"

Having had some spring last week I began on my Lark Theme. Having settled them all down busily and noisily writing stories, feeling keenly myself the spring in the air, with the sun pouring across the prefab through the generous windows, I ran over to the piano and began playing "Hark, Hark, the Lark!" Then something happened which is the highest peak of achievement in what I, for want of the real words, call my teaching.

Whether it was the genius of Schubert speaking over the century through his inspired music, whether it was what I myself felt as I interpreted his music, whether it was the spring in the air after the unprecedentedly cold winter or whether it was ripe to come anyway, it came.

There was a flash of yellow to my right; I looked around. It was Twinnie dancing. I thrilled violently. It was not hula or any native dance. It was a fine, exquisite expressive dance, such as is cultivated these days as something new but which belongs to the days before time. It was perfectly in rhythm with the music and followed the feeling of it. Up floated the other Twinnie. They danced to each other, from each other, their arms expressing, their hands and their small bodies. Two small brown spirits with bright yellow jerseys like jonquils.

Sometimes life is on our side. Believe it or not, there was a loaded camera on the table.

"Get this, Colleen!"

But there was no hurry. Ronald got up and Matawhero, the little Tamati girls, Riti and Hine, and there was the loveliest sight I have seen. Swaying, dipping, whirling to the spring music of Schubert.

They had never heard this music before. They had never danced in that wonderful way. It was purely spontaneous. Purely *organic!*

I gave all the flowers to Schubert. But I kept one myself for a crown.

I remember now though that the camera was on "simultaneous" and not "time." So they'll be blurred. But no, that was right, wasn't it? Colleen took the camera into Taradale tonight, I mean the film.

"Yesterday," I told the Head over lunch, "Tom gave my Tamati baby a hiding."

"What for?"

"For not obeying him. Think of it. The Tamati baby obeying anyone. The Tamati children are trained to disobedience from birth. You can tell that by their compositions as well as their behaviour. I've been very carefully bringing that baby round to a tentative obedience. Winning his confidence. As wild and shy as an opossum. And as charming and soft."

Tom told me this himself over lunch the previous day.

"A Tamati," I replied, to cover what I felt, "can obey neither God nor man. Let alone teacher." Then I was so angry that I changed the subject.

He gave Matawhero a hiding too. For saying "Cheat." A word that is outlawed in the school. But I had not warned the primers of this. Matawhero has been too good since; concentrating on things too hard for him and so on. You know what I think of my own mistakes over this boy. Even though his compositions tell of hidings at home.

Before I leave the unpleasant subject of Mrs. Cutter I'll tell you how both these little white boys, Dennis and Mark, live down the same road, a mile apart. Four times a day the Cutter car comes to the gate to bring and take Mark. The Woods car comes twice. Yet never can these two white families converge in the same car. It's not Dennis' family who stands in the way.

This morning I began teaching them the words of "Hark, Hark the Lark!"

"Hark, hark, the lark," I began.

But Mark was walking heavily across the floor with his plated shoes on. They repeated after me.

"Cluck, cluck, the lark!" and "Hark, hark, the clerk!"

Note to Colleen:

Colleen, I won't be there today. Would you give Tame the old blue Maori book in a blue box on the bookshelf in the storeroom so that he won't be disappointed. Please avoid the haka today as it rouses them and besides I keep it for special occasions. I'm returning the compositions they began on Friday to finish, if they can still remember what they had been thinking about. We are very short of paper. Would you please arrange a meeting of the C team at playtime and talk to them about yellow jerseys on Wednesday. It will be better for you to have story and drawing after lunch. The theme is still "Cluck, cluck, the lark." Thank you for all that.

Tomorrow are the provincial primary-school basketball championships in Hastings involving dozens of teams. After pulling down last year's winners, Paki Paki, a fortnight ago, I have been indisposed ever since and have taken no practices. But I didn't worry. They're just as alert and alive, I thought, and they know their combination. However I took myself to school today, only on account of tomorrow and ran them through a practice. And lo! What had happened! In the interim they had been playing at the pa, systematically undoing all that I had taught them, in technique and care and speed, so that today I nearly fainted to see the result. It was all gone.

Sadly I told this to the others after school. "I had thought," I told them, "that we might have picked up something tomorrow. But, take my word for it, we won't. All is lost."

WE

WON

THE

COMPETITIONS.

Into a group of over a thousand girls dressed in navy-blue uniforms on about a quarter of a mile of courts I let loose twenty-seven Maoris in brilliant yellow pullovers and dark-brown rompers. Like a stream of molten gold they poured down from the pavilion and made their fluid way through the crowds to courts 3 and 4 towards the other end. Nine of these yellows were destined to work their way back through the afternoon and through the courts as they progressively won and eliminated the others, to, finally, before the pavilion, at the end of the afternoon, win the finals.

Who is this yellow? one hears on all sides.

It was my modest A.

I had no voice. "Ronda," I whispered, "call out 'Come on Fernhill!' "

"Come on Fernhill!" she shrieked.

"Netta! Polly! Lotus! Call out 'Come on Fernhill!' for me."

Shrieks! Shrieks! Shrieks! "Come on Fernhill! Come on Fernhill!"

But my A was playing its fifth match on end without a break. They were exhausted and were, in true pa style, losing their tempers, not to mention losing the game. I ran onto the court when the desperate, furious play came

165

near. "Della," I whispered, "stop the long throws!"

I followed the ball down to the goal. "Take your time, Tatu!" as she aimed.

They were catching up. Somewhere I remembered that there was a rule against coaching from the sidelines. But I'm born for just that. To break anything in the way of a rule I encounter. Coach from the sidelines? I was coaching on the court. "Jean! Tatu! Leave out Ronda! Do the goal on your own!" They all must have heard my whispering.

It was almost Time, the referee was frightfully on the other side, and we were still behind. Then Kahu arrived running. They saw him. They heard him. "Look where you're throwing, Paulette!" they heard him say.

Three goals were scored in quick succession to catch and pass by *one* the others. The whistle went. . . .

It would have been an easier victory but for two things.

1. Brilliant Marion had an un-walk-on-able leg and was absent.

2. All the referees but one were against the "terrible Maoris."

I believe it was the appearance of Kahu that got them over the last fence.

I came home thinking, Now I'll stay home and go to bed until I am better; but K. showed me a letter from the Inspectorate saying,

"Your school will probably be visited for inspection purposes during the week commencing 13th August."

So now I must compose my new reading scheme containing all my newest and latest findings, mounted on good paper and bound, with reference to experiments, also complete the composition and making of the Maori primer, Ihaka Book Three, and *try* to do Book Four.

The organic behaviour.

Spontaneous dancing. There is more music in these children than flesh and blood. That is what I mean by "abstract organic pattern of behaviour."

By *organic* I mean that way of growth where the strongest thing pushes up ahead of the less strong. I think of trees growing in a clump. The strongest get to the light. In speaking of a child's mind I mean the strongest impulses push up, irrespective of whether or not they should, at a given time. Making the behaviour of the children anything but an ordered one in the conscious meaning of the term *order*. I call it the abstract order because the pattern it makes is so mixed up, so unpredictable. That's how I come to relate the terms *abstract* and *organic*. They are associative. *Natural* includes them both.

That's what I wish I could have, but I wonder. That man Neil in England ran a school like that. But I don't want it as bad as that. When my children broke into dancing the other day—they still do—and when Seven picks up the axe . . . I seem to see it. When my Tamati baby just doesn't do what he's required to . . . the movement, the talk, the silences uncalled for, the running to

the door at a knock, the loud crying, the spontaneous singing, the composition . . . it makes an abstract pattern *because* the behaviour is organic.

They were due this week, the Inspectors. Now it's Wednesday morning, twenty to nine. I'm very nervous. I wasn't on Monday, and not so bad on Tuesday, but now I'm worn out. I've still got my white jersey on with . . . I mean in which I meet bad situations. It's been hard to keep it clean for three days. I've cleaned the white soles of my black shoes every morning for three mornings, a thing I never do, and I've worn all my Maori belts. It's no good anybody telling me not to be nervous. There's a ghoul from the past that haunts, I think, all teachers of my generation, from those five-year-old days when we felt the tension of the teacher and the foreboding of the Inspector himself. I can't recall at this moment the care Mr. T. has put into the handling of me for the last eighteen months, his diligence in encouragement and his determination to win my confidence. It all goes down before the ghoul of the past. If *only* I had the confidence of being a good teacher. But I'm not even an appalling teacher. I don't even claim to be a teacher at all. I'm just a nitwit somehow let loose among children. If only I kept workbooks and made schemes and taught like other teachers I should have the confidence of numbers. It's the payment, the price of walking alone. If you saw the reading scheme I have been making the last few days you'd know why I speak of walking alone. Yet I must present it. I've got to do what I believe. And I believe in all I do.

It's the price one continually pays for stepping out of line. I'm feeling too old to pay it. But I *must* do what I believe in or nothing at all. Life's so short. What other people call their timetables. . . . In mine, the children might get up and dance in the middle of their sums. Matawhero might stand up and lead a haka if I'm not careful. Oh dear. Edmund Burke. Stay with me today.

1 P. M. There are times when I can't teach and this is one of them. There are troughs in effort as well as peaks and this is one of them. There's a lot of noise, a lot of coloured chalk, a lot of music, a lot of reading, some singing and laughing, but a trough nevertheless it is for me.

I'm not one of those souls like drifting rain-wraiths out of touch with the essence of life, looking backward through thick tears at some moment departed and weeping that life is not worthwhile. I use those moments. At each of those times I saw the meaning of life and knew that I saw it. True, I knew that inevitably there would be many deep troughs to follow. But every time I reached those heights I said, "All my life before and my life after is justified by the wonder of this moment." Many of those moments I have forgotten now but I haven't forgotten what I said. And I trust myself. Whatever comes my way now, I know already that it has been worth being alive. Even in troughs like this.

A dear friend wrote to me this week saying, "I must make a fight through these forties. The beginning of the end of life—and all my life I have been waiting, waiting for life. When I think of what might have been I know that it is time for another tablespoon of my medicine."

But I know that he has had his share of heights.

Another dear friend tells me that since the glow of the past has gone he is truly dead. "If I can't have that," he said, "then why live?"

Well, even Freud said, "Life is not much, but it's all we've got."

I know that in my past a lot has gone by too. But it *did* happen. It *was* there. And at those times I was sure that everything in life was justified. I see life sometimes as a bird flying. I see a soul on the wing through a trackless storm, and every now and again there is a lull and the bird comes to rest on land. Those contacts with the earth

before departing into the storm again I see as the moments in life when I knew the meaning. And even though between them I have my share of storm with everyone else, I am comforted always by the knowledge that there *is* land below, because I have seen it. I am inspired to go on because I have seen the meaning myself.

As I grow older the moments do not lessen so much as change character. As one matures, the fusion with other souls graduates into fusions with life. I know this when I wake in the morning and see through the window the black macrocarpa against the early morning sky and realise that I am still alive. It's an ecstasy no less than a moment of love, but different. It holds the same flash of realisation, the same acute pain and the same inspiration. When I was younger, more devout and more symbolic in my thinking, I used to say, "I have seen God's face." Whether it is God's face or not I see something. And whatever it is, it justifies breath. . . .

When Keith brings my tea early in the morning I pull myself up on my pillows, stare through the aperture of the curtains of the far window to see the pattern of the black tree against the tender, new sky, then turn and jerk back the curtain from the window behind me to see the garden, the fields across the road, the hills in the distance and the shadowy mountains. Just to make sure, *sure,* that it is all true, that I am really part of all this amazing living and that there is yet another day.

Thursday morning. I know now why they haven't come yet. My Scheme was incomplete. I thought of de Maupassant's lovely thought as I was sitting with my feet in hot soapy water to comfort and compose myself a few minutes ago.

"Words have souls. But that soul is not manifest until its word is graciously set."

So there it is at the beginning of my Reading Scheme. And I feel better. There's a reason for everything. So they'll be here this morning for sure.

I washed my white jersey last night and cleaned my white soles this morning for the fourth time running and once more wished K. good luck as he left for school.

"I haven't had a letter from Waiwini yet in Health

Camp," said Colleen. "She promised she would. It was the very last thing she said to me."

"Do you want to know her last words to me?"

"What?"

"She said, 'You've got a long chin!' "

Wiki: I frighteen of the skellington. He got plenty bones.

Seven: I'm frighten of the worms.

Larry: I'm frighten of the ghosts.

Betty: I'm frighten of the ghost. It eat all us up.

Wiki: I'm frighten of the ghost. I shoot the ghost. It jump on my back.

Rangi: I frighten of the police. They kill me with the butcher knife.

Mare: I frighten of the fire engine. It burn me up dead.

Betty: I frighteen of the ghost. It eat all us up.

Friday morning and the last day of the term.

"Do you really think," I said to the Head as he left for school at his regular eight o'clock, "that they will come today? The last morning of the term, and raining?"

"I can't help thinking but what they will acknowledge their appointment."

I'm not cleaning the white soles of my black shoes this morning, and the cuffs of the white jersey are not white. I haven't opened my Reading Scheme for one last anxious look, and the week's ironing is only half done. I didn't even wish K. good luck as he left. I'm not insensitive to rhythm.

And I'll forgive Mr. T. for the unnecessary week of tension for the school, the soles cleaned four times running and the jersey washed in mid-week. I'll even forgive him for the pressure of the completion of the Reading Scheme. Who am I to question organic behaviour in Inspectors, I who preach it?

But I can't forgive him for the ironing not being finished and I'll never wear the white jersey again.

In accordance with a promise in the fever of victory on the day of the basketball competitions I am, tonight, taking the A team to the pictures, may God in His mercy preserve me. It seems that we are going to see some Warner Brothers spectacle in ravishing colour called "The Flame and the Arrow." May God in His mercy, I repeat, preserve me and bring me safely through.

Holidays

I must get this off my mind before I indulge in anything else. I met Mrs. Cutter in town recently and as she passed me she looked into a shop window and she turned Mark's face away too so that he should not see me. What made it worse was that I had a Maori companion with me: anathema to Mrs. Cutter.

The first thing Mark did when he returned to school after the holidays was to wait for me on the step (I was late), and when I went in to sit down he stood by me and held both my hands for some time.

I made a Maori belt for my cream coat with which to dazzle Wellington last week. It was a red, cream and black rafter-pattern from Porourangi, the meeting house at Waiomatatini, the darling of Sir Apirana Ngata's heart and the most comprehensive and spectacular meeting house in New Zealand. Everyone could not help but notice the belt, which made it very hard to wear. But only a few recognized its import: part of the advent of the New Zealand native culture at last into the European. It pacified me that it should be recognized for what it was in the higher rungs of thinking. It was, indeed, more than noticed. It received an emotional ovation. Not in the streets of course. There it was only something unusual and of an untoward brightness and something unrelated to what one sees in the shop windows. But in the informed areas, behind closed doors, it was acknowledged for what it was. Part of the Mighty Birth. The blended culture.

But even apart from that, its import, they loved it for the looks of it; for itself without the weight of its respon-

174

sibility. And how I needed all this support. I did. I did. It called on more courage to wear this belt than it has done to wear anything else. But something unnameable, something irresistible and coming from the center of me, forced me to wear this belt about Wellington. But the trial of doing so was balanced. By what? By stray Maori eyes finding it. That was a prize! The way the little Maori girl in Woolworth's served me! You should have seen her. I might have been her most desired warrior. The friend who was with me was quite fascinated. And a middle-aged Maori waitress just put down her plates and stopped in her tracks, and the way two young Maori men standing on the far corner suddenly decided to cross the street and pass me closely! Lambton Quay those spring mornings became a heady adventure.

Well, here I am at the end. I have had Tom in my room giving demonstration lessons in writing. They are excellent lessons and Colleen and I learn much.

My little white Dennis is in a nursing home with a nervous breakdown. Plunket* upbringing and a young ambitious mother bent on earning more and more money. She beats him with a stick. In my word experiments he told me he wasn't frightened of anything except the sky. But his mother said he was afraid even of the chickens. I have a burning desire to pick up some of my neurotic whites and keep them for a while. My white June (Plunket) is still on holiday, which I advised.

The traffic inspector was out here the other day wanting to know why our children rode their bikes across the footway of the large new bridge here and yet walked on the traffic way. There are many questions about our children that we can't answer.

Professor Baillie said the other day, "Tidiness kills education."

I said, "Say that again."

"Tidiness," he repeated for me, "kills education. I'm a very untidy person myself."

* *Plunket:* a method of child rearing, successful physically but disastrous psychologically. Lord Plunket, Governor General of New Zealand about 1906, gave his name to this method.

"We have no time to be tidy here. And all that material! The time it takes to find, and put away and look after! Give me a blackboard and chalk!"

So many teachers put the emphasis on appearance while the meaning is atrophied. I very seldom find good hand-writing going with a good head. My perfect writers are excellent copyists. But my real creative, artistic brains are failures with a pencil. Look at Matawhero. Him I place among the brightest and most sensitive beings ever to pass my way.

I am disturbed, though, to see the pages of unrelated sentences in newcomers. Presumably sentences containing certain words in current learning. That's bad. Those are the first lessons in disintegration. Writing must be cohesive. An integrated, developing idea. Every word presented must be part of a grand design. A necessary part. Every morning after a period of free conversation my Little Ones, right down to the fives, write of something close to them. The words they use are words of *their* choosing and are necessary to them and are part of the developing idea in their young minds. There is *sequence* in what they write, and intense meaning, since each child writes about that thing that is on his mind. Otherwise it's all teacher. Education, fundamentally, is the increase of the percentage of the conscious in relation to the unconscious. It must be a developing idea. None of this is new, of course. It's the understood design of today's education.

Hearing singing on the spring air before dinner tonight, I looked down towards the pa. And there on the *roro** of the meeting house was the youth club practising for the contest tonight. It was good singing. And very different from the singing we got recently during the holidays when there was a hockey tournament down there. Beer singing. (And all this was over a loudspeaker from the pa hall with three amplifiers on top of the roof.) But even that was all right in its exuberant way. The first day and the first evening. Even the whole night through the next morning and the next evening, it was at least bearable. But it was the second night, right through, that it showed signs of deterioration (they forgot to turn off the loudspeaker

* *roro:* verandah.

176

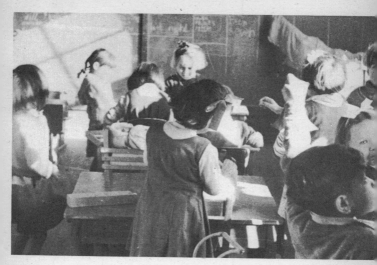

on the roof). And after having had to listen to it all night until the second morning I couldn't see anything in it at all. Yet I took all that, believing in live and let live, right through that day and that night. But the *third* morning, being mere Pakehas, we had no more endurance left.

Hockey! What a joke! A mere excuse to get together. And by together, I mean just that. *Together.* All night and all day, in spirit and in body. A friend of mine attended two of these "hockey tournaments," but what I call "beer tournaments." They sing and drink all night. Till morning. Not that I don't know this. When we lived further from the Board we sang and drank just as well until morning on many an occasion, and these pa parties I have never seen equalled in any place and at any time of life. It's just that we didn't have three amplifiers on the roof.

Together. Maoris know all about fusion. The communal heart and the communal mind has not yet been wholly broken by the New Culture. I don't really quarrel with it. Beer and all. They might as well. One of the old drinking kuias said to me in Pipiriki, "I must have my happiness." I knew what she meant.

As for the police. They supply the beer! I'll stand by that. They do.

177

But every dark night has its star. I woke up one of these musical nights to a golden tenor through the clouds of sleep. It rose in height and volume until I was roused fully. It was Kahu. I opened my eyes. It was dawn. I closed them again. Kahu was not drunk. He was singing over the microphone down at the pa to what, by the sound, was a huge audience. This voice in the dawn was like a golden bird on the wing. Mounting, mounting *mounting!* It was some song I had not heard before. It rose to its climax and the end that is his own particular characteristic: a trill and a twist and last high note.

Its setting was a grand drunken debauch, but it is one of those moments that I'm going to count over again when I know death is near. Kahu in the dawn.

Now that the basketball is over we can pick up our orchestra again. The purpose of this is more social than musical. Understandably. Nevertheless a little music crept in. But more and better music will creep in this year. Everything has to begin somewhere. And this was a beginning.

When I teach people I marry them. I found this out last year when I began the orchestra. To do what I wanted them to do they had need to be like me. More than that. They had to be part of me. As the season progressed the lesson began to teach itself to me. I found that for good performances we had to be one thing. One organ. And physically they had to be near to each other and to me. We had to bundle into a heap round the piano. I say "we had to," but that's not it. They *did* pile up round me at the piano, irrespective of what I tried to make them do. However, I arranged their seating to face the audience and with a view to each child being visible; nevertheless, at the end of the song, there they would all be, married all over and round me.

Rules like the best sound coming from a throat or instrument when facing the auditorium were just walked over. Although I didn't learn that thing until I heard the . . . *saw* the youth club sing a lament at the tangi of Whareparita's twins. They were too shy to face the gathering, so instinctively, they turned inward into a ring, seeing

only one another. As for me, I learnt this particular lesson once and for all. I know it now.

Now where was I? I was talking marriage with my orchestra. I would never have learnt this through any other medium but music, I'm sure. I've never learnt it all this time teaching. But now that I do know it I see it in other areas. There is quietly occurring in my infant room a grand espousal. To bring them to do what I want them to do they come near me, I draw them near me, in body and in spirit. They don't know it but I do. They become part of me, like a lover. The approach, little different. The askance observation first, the acceptance next, then the gradual or quick coming, until in the complete procuration, there glows the harmony, the peace.

And what is the birth? From the orchestra it is music, and from the infant room it is work. A long, perpetuating, never-ending, transmuting birth, beginning its labour every morning and a rest between pains every evening.

Now that I see this as espousal the prickly, difficult, obscured way clears. It's all so simple.

Tall words. Wild words. Grand words. But there is an even deeper meaning beneath it all. It's integration of my living. And integration of theirs.

179

All the rules of love-making apply to these spiritual and intellectual fusions. There must be only two, for instance. As soon as another allegiance pushes in, the first union breaks apart. Love interferes with fidelities. I can't teach in the true essential medium when that approaching face turns away to another interest. I have tried in the past to do this, before I knew what I know now, but the answer was grating, discord, and even hatred. When love turns away, now, I don't follow it. I sit and suffer, unprotesting, until I feel the tread of another step.

Thinking of these things I can see wonders in the past that I had not realized at the time. I remember how much time I spent *talking* to my A team. Endlessly through the cold winter I had them in my room, on the mat before me or sitting on the low desks, discussing, working things out, fine points, big issues, behaviour, clothes and manners on the field. I didn't know then what I was doing, that I was deep in a fertile espousal, not even when they played their way to the top of the province. But I do now. I do now.

Integration. That fatal, vital word continues to press upward before the inner eye. Married to the life about you. However small or however big the social horizon. For the environment at hand has little bearing on the expansion of the mind and spirit. "Accident of dwelling-place does not necessarily mean parochialism of the soul." The features of the countenance of Life are the same. There is jealousy, pity, envy, compassion, joy, death, industry and peace just the same. It's just as possible to live to the full in a narrow corner as it is in bigness. Irrelevantly Flaubert comes to mind. Maybe that is why he died in apoplexy too early. He wrote and created out and beyond his own small home town. But, you will answer, what about *Madame Bovary?* It was outside the intellectual horizon of Normandy. And think of the disintegration of writing *Salammbô!* Ah well . . .

I'm glad I know this at last, that to teach I need first to espouse. And in coming upon this at last I find myself in a not undesirable company. I remember André Gide: "When I am alone I feel that my life is slowing down, stopping, and that I am on the very verge of ceasing to exist. My heart beats only out of sympathy; I live only

through others—by procuration, so to speak, and by espousals; and I never feel myself living so intensely as when I escape from myself to become no matter who."

In essence Yeats speaks the same conviction: writing to a fellow worker in the building of a new Ireland, "the test of one's harmony is one one's power to absorb the heterogeneous and make it harmonious. Absorb Ireland and her tragedy and you will become the poet of a people, the poet of a new insurrection."

The word "marry" is interchangeable with his word "absorb."

As for Buber, the German, he speaks of teaching as the "pedagogical intercourse."

These men have their different characteristics of expression: but to me the core of thought is the same: I teach through espousal.

I've got so much to say that I'm going to stop trying to

say it. This is the last lot of this diary. The level of it is rising over my head.

Its purpose has been already fulfilled. I was lonely, professionally. I wanted gifted, intimate understanding. I've had it. I'm no longer professionally lonely.

Before I stop I'll try to cover the very vital and organic pattern of my professional life over the last weeks. It's always when things happen that we have no time to record them. But I'll try to give the picture, the conglomeration of imagery that has been banking up before the inner eye, waiting and pushing for expression. And the order will be its own. An order of emotional importance.

Stronger than any other image in the world behind is one of Mr. Tremaine in my infant room last week saying to me softly, "I want to hear you speak." Through everything else I hear this. Right through the Ballet on Thursday evening, the evening of his visit, I heard this. True, he had brought with him Professor ——— from the chair of ——— and Dr. ——— from the chair of ——— at ——— University College to meet me, but it was this modest sentence of Mr. Tremaine's that remains the strongest thought within. The strongest sensation.

He kept from me who the visitors were. They had come to see my Maori primer books. They got me talking, Mr. Tremaine did, and these two men I lectured from the infant-room table with all the fire of conviction I had in me on the results of my recent experiments with the Key Vocabulary. I'm not going into these findings here since they are all presented in my Maori Infant Reading Scheme which is now looking for a publisher.

"The way," I reproved Mr. Tremaine at morning tea in the ugly old porch, "you come out here and make me talk. You make me talk! I talk everyone down for an hour, then feel ashamed of it afterwards!"

He smiled in enjoyment. "I always find," he told us, "that if I keep quiet I learn something."

"Are you important?" I asked the visitors.

"Oh no, no!"

"Well, as long as I know. I would have passed you your tea first. Anyway Mr. Tremaine, I like your technique of dropping important people on us. If I knew they were coming I'd never be here!"

182

He roared at this and I wondered what for. Some secret interpretation he had. But as he shook my hand goodbye in the porch I said, "I'm attacking Maori delinquency."

"Thank you for all the work you are doing," he replied. "And I enjoyed listening to you."

That was the day I gave him my Maori Infant Reading Scheme. He stood in the cold outside, so very big and tall in his greatcoat, turning over the pages, and dwelling on de Maupassant's lovely thought. He put his finger on the schematic drawings of Ihaka with which I had introduced it. "Look at this," he said tenderly. Ah, the simple rapture of fulfilment at my work being understood that cold morning. What unutterable reward for my labour.

Remembering

—a story

What is it, what is it, Little One?

I kneel to his level and tip his chin. Tears break from the big brown eyes and set off down his face.

That's why somebodies they broked my castle for notheen. Somebodies.

I sit on my low chair in the raftered prefab, take him on my knee and tuck the black Maori head beneath my chin.

"There . . . there . . . look at my pretty boy . . ."

But that's only a memory now. A year old.

"Is Mr. Henderson in?" asks a man's voice at the other end of the phone in the evening. It is a year later. And I *did* resign.

"He's over at school, sir," I reply. "He'll be back at nine. Can I take a message? It's Mrs. Henderson speaking."

"Oh, I was just wondering about my floor in the new infant rooms, Mrs. Henderson."

"You're the man doing the floor in the new infant block?"

"Yes. Randall's my name."

"Well, it's not dry yet, Mr. Randall, from what I hear. The children didn't go in today. The Head couldn't let them go in. It was still sticky. The coat you put on is not dry yet."

"The children didn't go in! It's not dry yet!"

"The Head lit the two new stoves at six this morning, hoping to dry the air. But it's still sticky. Of course the teachers have been in on their stockinged feet. Would stockinged feet hurt it?"

"Oh no, stockinged feet wouldn't hurt it. You see, it's this weather. There's no drying. The men have told me that coats of varnish they have put on days ago have not

184

set. There's no drying at all. That's bad about the children not being in."

"It's worse than you think, as a matter of fact. The Inspectors are visiting the school on Thursday and Friday, and here are these young teachers breaking their necks to get settled. Such a big change-over and reorganisation moving into the new rooms. And they can't even have their children in."

"It's because there's no drying, Mrs. Henderson. There's no drying at all this weather."

"I know all too well there's no drying. My clothes have been on the line for days and I finally had to dry them inside."

"Things always happen at once. Like this."

"Of course, Mr. Randall, I don't know what arrangements the Head has made with his teachers, but possibly they have arranged to go in tomorrow. What with the fires going all day. And the Little Ones could sit on the mats."

"The children could go in with their socks."

"Socks? That's just it. I doubt if there's more than half a dozen socks between them. Would bare feet hurt?"

"No. Bare feet wouldn't hurt."

"They took the furniture in today though. The chairs and tables."

"Oh, you know how children wiggle round on their chairs!"

"They'll probably sit on the mats."

"Yes, they could sit on the mats."

It's not often I put nylon stockings on in the morning now. In fact that's one of the things I resigned about: putting on nylon stockings in the morning for school when other women turned up in their slippers to do the ironing. But this morning I do. And powder my face and tie my hair back with a ribbon. Just as in the mornings a year ago when I would trail over an hour after the Head to school to share his work. I want to see my Little Ones go into the new infant block. With or without socks. With or without me. While they are all still gathered in assembly outside I too take off my shoes at the door and go in on the marvellous floor in my stockinged feet.

You should see these new rooms! They might have come straight off the easel of my Little Ones a year ago, except that they have no legs. Wiki and Mohi always painted legs on their houses. All colours! Even outside. Areas of yellow here, blue higher up, red doors . . . can you believe that such imagination and understanding of a Little One could have come out of the dark back rooms of a school architect? Inside there are rows of little cupboards of every colour known and unknown to God and Man. The colours on the panels of the walls might have been painted by Maori five-year-olds themselves. Above the blackboards on one end there is wallpaper of nursery rhymes; on the other, cowboys and Indians. Think of it—wallpaper in an infant room with cowboys and Indians! The ceiling is softly lit yellow, the stays a deeper primrose. One entire wall facing the north is glassed, showing the walnut tree right here that the architect insisted should not be taken out. Plainly this architect has lifted the whole thing from the pages of a children's picture book; or helped himself to the ideas on a ten-child easel. My mind is quite hushed with respect.

The kids like it and I like it, he told the Head recently, and that's all that matters.

But the floor! Is it a mirror on its back? It reflects

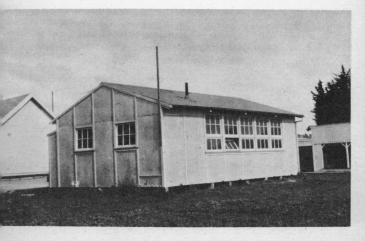

everything about and above it. Multiplying the million colours. What an artist that dear chap on the phone was last night. This floor was his darling.

I'm longing for my Little Ones to come in from assembly. A long long time since I have seen them. As I wait I move in awe over the floor into the next room and look out through the whole-wall window to where the prefab used to stand and where its site is now no more than a small oblong area of earth in the surrounding grass.

I see again in mind my rickety raftered rocky prefab that spilt the melting frost in the spring. With Sammy Snail wandering down upon us from the rafters, the sun thick tangible bars across the rising dust from the bare floor boards, the loud ever-moving, ever-talking life of the young of the New Race, from corner to corner, from wall to wall, both on the floor and upon the desks. Tall towers rocking precariously, fantastic shapes in colour leaping from the ten-child easel, Little Ones in eddying figures of dancing, the clay-births, the sand turning into a graveyard under passionate brown fingers, the water trough with one-pint building wharves, bombers zooming on the blackboards, outrageous statements in funnily spelt words on the low wall blackboards, children singing, quarrelling, magnificently, laughing for nothing, infec-

tiously, crying for nothing infectiously, Waiwini's Little Brother wailing to me that somebodies they broked his castle for notheen. Bleeding Heart laughing his head off, the Tamatis' dog snuggling about for a cuddle, Pussy insinuating herself fastidiously, the Ginger Rooster scratching about ambitiously for culture, pictures of the meeting house and pa and the Ghost and of big-footed people kissing and words like shearing shed and beer and graveyard and wild piggy and lollies, tongues patrolling Maori lips over intensely personal writing, voices raised in exuberance, in argument, in reading, laughter, singing and crying and How-do-you-spell-Nanny. And our *floor!* You should see our floor! Round about the ten-child easel where the colour drips, it's prettier than the face of the countryside itself. You'd think Autumn himself had passed this way with his careless brush; slinging his paint about in his extravagant way. And noise . . . noise! And the whole show rocking like an overcrowded dinghy on high seas.

"What is it, what is it, Little One?" I hear myself again.

"That's why somebodies they broked my castle for notheen; somebodies."

There . . . there . . . look at my pretty boy. . . .

Here they come!

The young teacher stands at the door. She's got a mind of her own, a face of her own, a style of her own and a voice. She's all there; contained and integrated. She stands at the door in slippers.

Now anyone who has shoes take them off, she says, and come in quietly. Don't push the tables and chairs. You'll scratch the floor. Bring your bags and shoes over this way to the porch and I'll show you where to put them.

I stand back by the new stove and watch them come in. They are all new, the faces of these babies. The Head hasn't warned me of this. Just the very Maori ones are left who can't read the imported books: One-Pint, Blossom, Bleeding Heart and Nuku. I watch them filing in. Pussy should appear any time now. She was on the Roll. Where is the Tamati's dog? Has he gone elsewhere for his canoodling? And Ginger Rooster . . . don't tell me he's left school! And whatever would Sammy Snail think

of these modern ceilings? I follow them all quietly in my own stockinged feet. The floor man who rang last night would be proud of us.

In the porch the teacher has put dear little pictures by each coat hook for identification. I look at them eagerly. Monkey, sailor boy, animals, and children with white skin and shoes and tidy hair and carefully ironed clothes. I look anxiously for pictures from the pa, the meeting house, Nanny, Wild Piggy, for brown children with bare feet and black hair. . . .

I move silently, more silently than Mohi's ghost, into the second room of the upper primers . . . it takes two teachers and two new rooms to meet the requirements. . . . Here I should find my Little Ones of a year ago. I do. All bigger! But why don't they run to me and throw their arms round me and carry my pen-box and coloured chalk, and why does not Waiwini's Little Brother wail to me that somebodies they broked his castle for notheen; somebodies? They rise in a body, silently. "Good morning, Mrs. Henderson."

"Now, Wiki," says the charming little girl teacher gently, "you show us how you can sit in your chair without scraping the floor."

Where are they going to put the easel? I wonder. What about the sand? What'll happen when they bring the water trough in? But they haven't brought them in. The little teacher has already put up some of her charts. Excellent presentation of printed words, in alphabetical order, from the imported books. I look hurriedly to the P list for "pa." But it's not there. Hurriedly, falling over my own mind, to the M list for "meeting house." No meeting house. N? No "Nanny." K? No "kiss." G? Where's G? Where's G? Have they got "Ghost?" No, they haven't got "Ghost." Not our Ghost. That so haunts and dominates and disorganises the Maori mind from the past Maori constabulary of the Gods. No . . . no Ghost. One-Pint and Bleeding Heart would have been put up by now on their own organic vocabulary. They would have been able to read by now. But what lovely clean orderly printing anyway. Far better than any the children themselves could have done.

One last look at the baby room before I slink silent-footed out. The teacher is still introducing them to their pictures on the coat hooks. It's time to go now. I look across the shining floor through the wall-length windows, past the nearby walnut tree to the earth side of the prefab. It really is true that it has gone. It's just absolutely not there. Yet that rocky, raftered little barn with its melting frost and its vociferous company had housed my own castle; the Key Vocabulary that I had built as spontaneously as any of my Little Ones; block on block precariously, turret on turret dangerously, with archways, stairways and defending cannon . . . and now all I can see through this elegant modern windowing is an area of earth in the grass.

I deliver one of my historic sighs, and turn within. All is sanity and silence and floor. I try to say something. After all I am the Head's wife and the former infant mistress. Think of how apt and encouraging a thing I could say. The Little Ones are still fondling their hooks wordlessly, their elegant and competent young teacher talking to them. I do try to say something. But my throat swells in that way when I see brown eyes when somebodies they break their castle for notheen; somebodies. It jams and I can't make it work. So I turn and move to the door, pull on my shoes and make my way back through

190

the coloured trees and over the wet ground, splashed in a holocaust of autumn colour as though my Little Ones had been painting here.

I plug in the jug from habit when I return to the kitchen and go unnecessarily to the mirror to check my hair that I have washed this morning. Sparkling five-year-old tears on an autumnal face.

That's why somebodies they broked my castle for notheen; somebodies. . . .

Nor all your tears wash out a word of it. . . .

ABOUT THE AUTHOR

SYLVIA ASHTON-WARNER has taught for twenty-four years in a Maori school in New Zealand, where she now lives. She is the author of numerous highly acclaimed novels, including *Spinster, Incense to Idols, Greenstone* and *Bell Call.*

Miss Ashton-Warner's articles have appeared in many magazines.